I Changed Gods

by Maria Anne Hirschmann

PACIFIC PRESS PUBLISHING ASSOCIATION

Mountain View, California

Omaha, Nebraska

Oshawa, Ontario

This book is dedicated to the young people of America and to my children Chris, Mike, Hanna, Maryanna, and JoJo, who are proud to be American youth.

I am deeply grateful to Pacific Union College and my many student friends; to Chris, my oldest daughter; and to my patient husband for their help and encouragement while I prepared the manuscript for this book.

May the narration of this story glorify only one name: Jesus Christ.

Library of Congress Catalog Card No. 68-29918

Contents

Good-bye, Mother!

My train whistled shrilly, and the sound echoed along the narrow streets of the ancient village. I stood at the open train window smiling down into the sad, blue-gray eyes of my aged mother.

There she stood on the station platform, her tired shoulders slightly bent, her thin white hair combed straight back into a tiny braided bun, her small, slender figure looking forlorn and wind-blown in an early-morning breeze.

For centuries the people of my homeland, the Sudetenland in Czechoslovakia, have struggled to wrest a living from the mountain soil, and the battle for survival has furrowed their faces and their hearts. They are sparing of words and diffident in display of affection. But now that I was leaving home, Mother kissed me. She had kissed each of the other four older children when they left home. The same old train had taken them away from home and from Mother, and now I too was leaving, the last fledgling to leave the nest.

Now Mother would go back to her clean, friendly cottage beneath the cherry trees. Everything would be quiet for her, and peaceful—and empty. But things should go easier for Mother, and perhaps for Father too. They would not have to work quite so hard anymore. Maybe Father's health would improve, for his strenuous labors as a bricklayer and farmer had left him ill and bitter.

He and I had never been friends. He was a short, thin-faced man with a black mustache, wordless, harsh, often bending over with pain from a sick stomach; zealous for his church, but with

5

Looking back, I saw a lonely figure—my mother.

little love. His ideas of a patriarchal household, where the father must reign with an iron hand and where wife and children had to submit silently, clashed with my proud, unbroken young spirit countless times. He had tried to subdue me with a leather belt, and by making me go hungry. No, I had never dared to answer back when he scolded. I knew better. But my set jaw, clenched fists, and blazing eyes had signaled rebellion clearly enough. Often they had thrown him into fits of rage.

Poor little Mother! She had been the go-between for all those years, and the tongue-lashings she had endured so often for my stubborn sake had been my greatest and most painful punishments. Only her pleading, tearful eyes had been able to melt my rebellion—sometimes! Yes, I could do anything for her, even apologize.

I knew that my stubbornness had been poison for Father's stomach, and I had caused him a lot of extra pain. Now I was leaving, and I hoped sincerely that Father would relax and feel better, for Mother's sake.

I looked down at her calloused hands, with their knotty veins. For so many years they had planted, weeded, canned, cleaned, washed, ironed, scrubbed, harvested from dawn until late at night. I had never seen Mother in slow motion. The only quiet moments she ever had were during worship time or her personal devotions before bedtime. Now I was leaving, and Mother's hands could rest a little more. She might even be able to read her Bible in the afternoon, and I was glad for her.

The sooty steam engine started to hiss and smoke. Sparks and cinders flew into the clear, cool air over the train cars. I laughed, amused. This train was helping me fulfill a dream. I was going into the wide world. I knew little about it, but I was eager and willing to dare and go.

Not that it was easy to part from the little world of my childhood. I loved the old cottage, the warm hayloft where I had slept, the dark-green forest that came up to our back windows. I had spent countless happy hours gathering wild berries and mushrooms in the shady coolness of the evergreens. And there were my furry cats and my gentle goats, the bees, the blossoming fruit trees, the brook, the forget-me-nots I had picked for Mother —all this I loved. And, most of all, I loved Mother.

With my excitement and anticipation I felt sadness and a bit of fear and foreboding as I looked again into Mother's silent face, lined with hundreds of small wrinkles. Something puzzled me in Mother's countenance. Her eyes had the kind of deeply troubled look I had seen only once or twice before. Why should Mother look so worried? This was a happy moment. Yes, we were parting, but I was on my way to a great future and many honors, and she would someday be honored by it too! Wouldn't she?

The first time I had seen her so helplessly sad, I was still very young. I had been quarreling with Sepp, my brother three years older than I. He had been teasing me, as he so often did, till I lost my temper and began to hammer his back with my small fists, yelling and screaming at him.

Suddenly he had turned around and said, "Look, Sis! Save your breath and get lost! Don't you know that you aren't even my sister? I'm the real son here, and you are just a nobody, an orphan. My mother is not your mother either!"

I stared into his grinning face and shouted, "I am going right now and tell Mother what you said. And you are going to get into trouble!"

"Go and tell! She is *my* mother, not yours, you *Dummkopf.* Go ahead, tell her!" Sepp gloated.

Storming into the kitchen, I threw my arms around Mother and wailed, "Sepp is lying, isn't he, Mother? He said you are not my mother!"

She gently loosened my arms from her waist and said softly, "Marichen, your brother is right. I am not your real mother. Your mamma died when you were just a little baby. Before she went to sleep she brought you to my house and laid you over there on the wooden bench beside the stove. We took you in. Your papa has never asked for you, never written. People say he's

7

married again. Now you are my girl, Marichen, and I will keep you!"

"Sepp," she said, turning to her son, "I do not think that Jesus was happy about what you did. It was unkind of you to say it the way you did too!"

That was the first time my world had broken apart. I sobbed into Mother's patched apron, while Sepp left the kitchen, apparently ashamed.

Mother stroked my blond, unruly hair, wiped my runny nose, and waited until my crying eased. Her eyes told me that she suffered with me. A shadow had fallen into both our hearts, but from that hour I learned to love her even more deeply.

The second time I had seen agony in her eyes was just a few months before I left home. War had begun in 1939, just a year after Hitler's troops overran Czechoslovakia. All the young men were called to bear arms. Sepp, Mother's youngest son, had been drafted too. We all were sad, but the parting was not really Mother's greatest concern. She knew that men must go to war. This was a pattern of life in Europe. Grandfather had fought in the Franco-Prussian War. Father served several years during World War I, just after he and Mother had married. Now it was Sepp's turn. But her greatest burden was that she had become an Adventist after the first world war and Mother did not want her sons to carry rifles and kill human beings. She feared Hitler would make no exceptions for Sepp, for Nazi rules were iron rules. She knew, too, that her thinking was considered dangerous and "braveless" in the eyes of the village party leader. "Heil Hitler" for everybody—that was it!

Sepp himself had not seemed disturbed about the matter as he made ready to leave. There were the daily radio announcements of victory from every fighting front, and he was young and strong and eager to help win the war. He looked sharp in his new uniform; and before he left, a girl in the village had whispered a sweet promise into his ear. The future belonged to him. After all, war would soon be over. But Mother seemed to know different, as she sadly bade her boy good-bye.

Now, why should Mother look at me in my hour of parting with the same helpless grief? I was not leaving to go to war. Didn't she realize how lucky I was, how happy and eager I felt? This was not a time of sorrow but of rejoicing, because I had been chosen from among many thousands of students to be further educated in one of Hitler's special schools. After many tests in school and special *"Führer"* camps I had been selected. It was a great honor. The village people envied us, and I bubbled with joy. Now I was leaving to go to the new Nazi school. Someday I would be a youth leader for the *Führer*. Why couldn't she rejoice with me?

The train began to move. Mother lifted her face, stretched out her hands toward me, and called, "Marichen, Marichen, don't ever forget Jesus!"

I smiled and called back, "Don't worry, *Mütterlein*, [Mother dear] how could I ever forget you and God?"

Why should Mother worry about such a matter? Hadn't she taught me to love God? Had I not prayed beside her from babyhood? Didn't I know my Bible? And what about the hymns we had sung together in our garden veranda and in church worship? To me God was like Mother, and Mother was like God. Whenever I prayed to my Friend Jesus, I could picture Him only with blue-gray eyes like Mother's.

The train gathered speed. In the receding distance stood a lonely figure waving a white handkerchief. Silhouetted against the bright morning sun, so fast she became smaller and smaller. I waved back to her, calling *"Auf Wiedersehen! Auf Wiedersehen!"* until the train rounded a curve and I saw her no more. The wheels as they rolled seemed to clatter, "Good-bye, Mother; good-bye, Mother; good-bye, village; good-bye, village."

The village left behind, I looked forward to the excitement of arriving in the city. My heart began to sing. Again I listened to the song of the wheels, and now they sang: "Let's go to Prague; let's go to Prague; let's go; let's go; let's go!"

9

I Changed Gods

The train pulled into the great railway terminal of Prague, and I stumbled down the steps to the platform. I could scarcely shake off the feeling that I was dreaming. Could it be true that I, the ignorant peasant girl from nowhere, was permitted to see Prague, the greatest city of my country? And I hadn't come just to visit, but to live and go to school in one of Hitler's new training centers. How could I be so fortunate?

We German young people called the city admiringly *Die Goldene Stadt* (The Golden City) after a popular color movie produced by the Nazis, which featured beautiful pictures of Prague. Now I had arrived! Dazed, I stood and watched thousands of strangers surge to and fro in the busy, crowded depot. How many people there were in this world! Holding tightly to my old suitcase and coat, I edged my way toward the gate, wondering in which language I should ask the conductor for the way to the streetcar. I spoke German, my mother's tongue, and Czech also. Knowing how deeply the freedom-loving Czech people hated the German regime and the German language, I was not sure what to do.

Timidly I approached a uniformed official and began to inquire of him in German. Then I quickly switched to Czech as I noticed resentment in his face. He gave me directions, and soon I found myself in a bench-like streetcar seat, looking curiously out the window.

What a long ride it turned out to be, almost through the entire city! But I didn't mind. As the streets and buildings flew past my window, I tried to recognize the historical places I had seen

10

in pictures; but I gave up after a while! It was simply too much. But I did see marvelous bridges and famous Hradčany Castle, 1,000 years old, silhouetted against the clear autumn sky. It seemed to me as if history itself stepped out of the printed page to welcome and greet me.

I soon decided which parts of Prague I loved the most: the "Old Town," an idyllic part of the original settlement dating back to the ninth century; Charles Bridge, over 1,600 feet long, dating from 1357, guarded by two massive towers adorned with statuary; the majestic Moldau River, the largest river of my country, spanned by twelve famous bridges.

"Mother Moldau" they call her because her waters mean fruitfulness and transportation for Bohemia. Unhurried, deep, and queenly she flows, carrying ships and boats under the old bridges, past flowery gardens and lovely parks.

I also saw sights of a different kind. As the antique streetcar rattled its way through the streets and beside the deep green river, Hitler's bright-red flags with the white circle and the black swastika waved in the autumn breeze from every great building and marketplace. The sidewalks were thronged with German soldiers, officers, and SS men, for the Czech "Praha" had become "Prag" and the city had changed its century-long traditions to please its German conqueror.

At last I arrived at my school, though it did not look like a school. The gate opened into a small park, beautifully landscaped with fountains and statuary. Large trees bordered the walks and the entrance to the main building. The school itself was a white stone mansion. Wide hand-carved wooden doors and slender high windows gave it the appearance of a castle out of a fairy tale. I half expected to wake up and find myself in my bed of straw, rubbing my sleepy eyes and feeling disappointed that it was only a dream.

After I had been registered and welcomed, I found my bed and *Spind*, as we called our wardrobes. Then I met some of my classmates. In the evening, feeling subdued and bashful, I sat

11

quietly in the luxurious dining hall where we were to receive three simple meals each day. I learned that the mansion was a confiscated estate of an immensely wealthy Jew. The idea disturbed me, but in the newness of my surroundings I dismissed these thoughts rather quickly. Someday I hoped to understand.

Before long I found myself well adjusted to my new way of life, and with youthful enthusiasm I faced my new opportunities. My shyness left me, and I bounced around as my usual overconfident self, ready to lead and to compete with the best of my class. I studied hard, learned to obey and salute in wordless submission, and soon received special recognition from the student body and faculty. I could forget that I had been an orphan girl dependent upon the mercy of a poor foster home; I felt accepted and needed.

Each day the memories of my childhood faded a little more. It seemed as if I had never lived any other life than my new Nazi school life. Mother seemed very far away and almost unreal.

How I loved school! My teachers could bring everything to life. History was fascinating. People long dead stepped out of the pages of my Nazi history book and lived again for me. They became my friends or enemies. They acted proud, heroic, or cowardly; they loved, fought, suffered, died. My vivid imagination lived and acted with them as my heart learned a new theme —"Adolf Hitler and the Third Reich." We young people who were in training to be Nazi youth leaders were Hitler's pride and joy. The *Führer* called us fondly *Das Deutschland von morgen* —the Germany of tomorrow. We loved this, and it seemed good and right to do his bidding.

Hitler was with us every hour, though he lived in Berlin and we in his school in Prague. His sayings were quoted in every class. His doctrines were our most important study. His *Mein Kampf* lay under the nightlamp on every bedside table. Our teachers worshiped him. They would undoubtedly lay their lives down for him and the nation. All our instructors were young, picked for their attitude, ability, and devotion to the party.

I Changed Gods

Though they demanded obedience and strict self-discipline, they were kind, warm, understanding, and fair.

But one teacher I loved above all others—our music teacher. Slim, petite, always smiling, tastefully dressed, she wore her hair in blond waves framing a pleasant oval face. Her main attraction was her eyes—big blue ones, true, firm, but understanding and kind.

Late one afternoon, several weeks after I had arrived at that school, I first decided Miss Walde was someone special. We had had an especially hard day, with many examinations. Our endurance had been tested, as it was so often, to our last limit. Our last test had been scheduled in the music room, and we marched into that place feeling played out and nervous. The girls urged me to be first to try the oral test. I complied, and stepped grinning up to the grand piano. The late afternoon sun flooded through the high windows and threw golden ornaments over my teacher, the instrument, and the soft Oriental rug beneath it. The dark-paneled room seemed dusty and hot. My teacher asked me to sing a German folk song for her, one we had studied a few days before. I had been braced for some difficult requirement, and her gentle request threw me completely off. I threw my hands before my face and burst into tears. Before I could compose myself, the whole group of girl students sobbed with me, not knowing what to expect next.

The teacher turned on her piano stool in surprise. She smiled reassuringly and then pulled a snow-white handkerchief out of her dress pocket and handed it to me. Deeply embarrassed over my emotional conduct, I dried my tears. Though I fumbled for it, I hadn't been able to find my own handkerchief.

When we had found our composure again, Miss Walde stood up and laughed sweetly. Then she said, "You are dismissed! Go for a walk in the sunshine, do anything you please, and report on time for supper."

"But—what about our music test?" I stammered. "Did we all fail?"

"Oh, no," she said reassuringly, "you all passed. Go out now and relax. We will have some more tests on another day."

Shouting our *"Dankeschön* [thanks]," we hurried out of the music hall and stepped into the afternoon sun. Separating myself from the group, I went to my favorite spot of the estate. It was a white bench nestled among large lilac bushes. Even though the lilac was not in bloom, I loved that place because it was a hidden, cozy place. Whenever I needed solitude for my dreams or problems I would go to "my" bench. Trying to bring order to my stormy, puzzled thoughts, I stared at the dainty white handkerchief still in my tense hand, and relived the last hour in the music hall. What a teacher! How good and noble she had been! How understanding and generous! What could I do for her to show my gratitude? I knew what she would say.

"Little Hansi," she would say, calling me by my nickname, "grow up pure and clean and give your life for the service of others, for our glorious Reich, and for *unseren Führer,* and it will be enough reward for me as your teacher."

Yes, I would do what she expected. I would grow up to be like her, firm and dedicated. Her blue eyes puzzled me. I could not escape the feeling that I had seen those eyes before I came to Prague. But where? And they were eyes I loved and respected. Where had I seen them before?

As time passed, Miss Walde and I developed a silent friendship. She could not show any preference to any student—that would have been unfair. But we both sensed that we were made to be friends. I studied hard for every subject, but music with her was a privilege, not work. She opened a new world to me. She slipped free tickets into my hand for concerts and opera. She lent me her books. She helped me over my stage fright when singing solos. She taught me the first steps in choir direction. Her blue eyes approved, disagreed, encouraged, and pushed. There was just one doubt in my mind, and that doubt perplexed me more and more urgently.

Among other subjects, we had one period daily of "Study of

Semitism" taught by a young SS *Offizier* who had been disabled
fighting in battle. Every day he hammered into our minds the
story of the Jews as the Nazi party saw it. Using *Der Stürmer,* an
anti-Semitic newspaper; Hitler's *Mein Kampf;* even the Bible, he
built his case against the Jews, maintaining that it was their
destiny to become extinct.

I listened attentively, and in my heart raged a battle. I had
been brought up with the Bible and prayer and faith in Jesus
Christ. Nobody had challenged them. Now, listening to this
teacher's convincing arguments, I was puzzled. Something was
wrong either with him or with me. I grew restless and uncom-
fortable as I tried to think the matter through. Miss Walde
noticed that I seemed perplexed, and raised her eyebrows in
silent question. I uncertainly shook my head; I could not talk
about it. It was so painful that I would not open my heart to
show the storm inside.

In the evening I climbed wearily into my bed and watched
the stars through the window. It had been a welcome diversion
when my roommates begged me to sing for them each evening.
We would retire more relaxed; and if we were lucky we would be
able to sleep through the entire night. Often we had to get up
as the air-raid sirens wailed; this was part of our life.

I had been used to praying before I went to sleep, and Mother
had taught me that prayer is talking to Jesus. But Jesus of Naza-
reth had been a Jew, and the Jewish people were condemned.
Now, why would the Son of the eternal God have to be a Jew
if those people were so bad? Didn't it show poor judgment on
God's part? If He was all-knowing, wouldn't He have seen that it
was a mistake? And could a modern Nazi student still pray to
that Jew, Jesus, without violating our code of living?

I lost weight. Food was not plentiful, and we lived on rations.
But even those small meals did not taste good to me, and I often
gave part of my food to my hungry roommate. I could often feel
the blue searching eyes of my favorite teacher rest on me, but
I dared not meet them.

15

I Changed Gods

One afternoon, having a few minutes free time, I had walked quickly to my favorite spot. As I approached the bench, I saw my teacher friend sitting there. Her face had become more serious lately, and her smile carried a hidden sadness. We all knew why!

She was engaged to an SS officer. I had seen his picture several times in her room. He was a tall, handsome young man with sparkling eyes, blond, curly hair, and a proud, sophisticated smile. He had been stationed in Prague several months, but now he had left for the front in Russia. Miss Walde was waiting for a letter, and we all waited eagerly with her. She was as sweet and efficient as usual, but behind her self-control and her smiles we knew she carried unshed tears.

I sat down quietly beside her and watched the windswept clouds. She didn't talk. I knew she was waiting for me to begin.

I turned to her and said haltingly, "Miss Walde, I'd like to ask you an unusual question. I hope you don't mind!"

She nodded, so I continued. "Do you think that a German youth can be a good Nazi and still pray as it was done in the olden days?"

"Maria Anne," she answered, "I appreciate your question. It shows me that you have a deep longing to do right. But there are two ways for us. The old way is the way of our parents, who live by their old-fashioned knowledge and will live by it until they die. But Hitler has been called by providence to show us young people a better and more scientific way. German youth have a calling, a task to do, for the Supreme Being and Hitler."

Miss Walde spoke persuasively. She shared her deep convictions. I knew she believed what she said.

Well, if she believed in the new religion, it was good enough for me. Yes, she believed in God too, only it was a different God, without the stain of Judaism.

"But what about prayer?" I asked.

She smiled again, and promised to give me a little book to read. It would explain everything, she said.

I Changed Gods

The title of the book was *Wanderer Between Two Worlds*. It contained the life story of the author, a well known Nazi writer. That evening I began to read it. From the beginning his style fascinated me, and I could hardly discipline myself to stop reading and take part in the evening activities.

Most impressive to me was his chapter on prayer. As a growing boy, the writer had decided to put God to a test. Taught by his mother to pray for protection, he one morning boldly decided not to pray, to see what would happen. As expected, the day went by without tragedy, and the next day. After a few days he dispensed with prayer for good. Then the author challenged the reader to try the same experiment and see what would become of old-fashioned, childish prayer.

I had tried it the next day, and it worked! I tried it the second day. Nothing happened. The book must be right. I was big and strong enough to take care of myself. That suited my independent, haughty spirit just fine. Dejection left me.

The only thing that bothered me was the thought of Mother. I could still see her at the train station with pleading eyes and hear her say, *"Marichen,* don't forget Jesus."

Mother would never understand my new way of life; she was set in her old beliefs. I didn't worry about Father. I had never cared for his concept of religion anyway; it had just made me rebellious. But I didn't want to let Mother down. But there was a new world in the making, a new ideology for young people; and the older people with their old-fashioned ways had to be left behind.

I read that book over and over again. I kept it beside my bed and memorized whole paragraphs. I lent the book to other young people and quoted its statements in letters to my friends. The book had shown me a new way of life. It meant victory, honor, fame, national pride. My last reserve had fallen. I had changed gods. I laid my burning heart and life upon the altar of my country—for Hitler.

I too had been a wanderer between two worlds. One world

17

was my mother's, the other my teacher's. Both women had the same eyes, the same great soul, the same kind heart, and I loved them both. But Mother's eyes spoke of resignation, patience, humility, while my teacher's eyes flashed with Nazi pride. The second way seemed better. I chose it and believed in it with all my heart. I trusted, believed, and followed; for Hitler had become our god, and we worshiped him. Hitler's war raged, and his youth were ready to die! He commanded, we obeyed. Heil Hitler!

The Unknown Sailor

For four years war raged. Air-raid sirens screamed at night. Refugees flowed endlessly through the city. The wounded crowded the military hospitals. War orphans multiplied. We kept more than busy caring for all these unfortunate people.

By 1944 our life had become a hectic tussle to fit studies in with volunteer service, night calls, emergencies, and a few hours of uneasy sleep. And added to this, gnawing hunger pains with weakness and dizzy spells. Wherever there was a need, we had to go; and we were glad to go. But sometimes our bodies could scarcely obey orders anymore.

The highlight of each school day was the arrival of the mailman. Mail was the only thing that was plentiful besides duties. I liked letters, and I liked to write. I would write in the bomb shelter at night, during class recess, whenever I could find an unoccupied minute. Almost daily I received a handful of mail from friends, including soldiers and officers. We knew how our boys waited for messages from home, and we all tried our best not to make them wait.

Mail did not always bring sunshine. Often it brought heartache. Often a letter addressed to a soldier would be returned to the sender stamped, *Gefallen für Führer und Vaterland* [Died for the Führer and fatherland]." How those few words under the name of the soldier would blow out the light in our hearts and eyes! Many of these boys had worked together with me in the Hitler Youth organization, and when they had left for military training and the fighting front, I had promised to write faithfully. I had kept my promises to all of them.

19

The first of my letters to be returned was one addressed to Fluntl, a friend of my early teens. A tall, blond youth, he had joined the SS troops. I had liked and admired him for his striking smile, his frank blue eyes, his bubbling enthusiasm, and his sincerity.

For weeks I couldn't believe he was dead. No, I didn't cry. A Nazi youth was not supposed to cry, for it was the highest fulfillment and greatest honor to die for our cause. I knew that Fluntl had believed in his calling and most likely had died with a *Heil* for the *Führer* on his lips. Was not self-sacrifice the greatest goal for any human being? Would tears not degrade his noble death?

I had controlled my tears, but I could not control the numbness in my soul. He had been the only son of aged parents. Why did he have to die? Why was life such a puzzle?

Several times my letters to soldiers came back with that fateful mark on them. Twice the stamp had been differently worded: "*Vermisst an der russischen Kampffront* [Missing at the Russian front]." This was more dreaded than the death note, for it spelled uncertainty, imprisonment, Siberia. It kept the people in the homeland in mental agony for years, hoping that in some way the missing boy might survive and return home.

Mail helped to keep the war going. As everybody knew, headquarters had ordered that in case of emergency, mail be delivered even if food was left behind. The boys could stand hunger as long as they had mail. And it worked both ways. How much easier it was for us to forget the meager lunch, the growling stomach, when we had interesting letters to read.

One spring day in 1942 I slipped out of class to receive my mail. Among other letters I noticed a long, dignified white envelope with strange handwriting on it. I couldn't make out the name of the sender. I checked the address again to make sure the letter was for me, and it was. I tore the envelope open and started to read. Then I sat down with an amused grin and called for a girl friend to come and see.

Well, who would have thought of that! Several months before,

The Unknown Sailor

Anneliese, my girl friend, and I had written letters addressed to an Unknown Soldier. Someone at Hitler's headquarters had started a campaign for more letter writing from the *Heimatfront* (home line) to the *Kampffront* (fighting front), and had suggested the writing to unknown soldiers. Since mail to the fighting forces had to be marked *Feldpost* (field mail) and did not require postage, the idea had caught fire. Almost everybody was writing to at least one unknown soldier.

On a rainy day Anneliese and I each wrote a letter to an unknown soldier, whom we imagined as a handsome, dashing hero. Since I liked the looks of our dark-blue-and-gold Navy uniforms best, and none of my friends had ever joined the navy (the normal choice for most of them was the SS), I had marked my dainty little letter "To an unknown sailor of the German navy." Then we had dropped our letters into the mailbox, laughing gaily with the excitement of the idea.

Nothing came of the letters, just as we had expected, and soon we dismissed the incident from our minds. From the beginning we had felt uneasy over it, anyway. It seemed strange to write a letter to a man without being asked by him. This didn't fit into our concept of etiquette or our strict code of proud womanhood.

Six months later I held the answer to my forgotten letter in my hand, and my curious classmates had kindly offered to help me decipher anything I couldn't read. Its writer must be a nice, polite man, intelligent, self-confident, and friendly, I decided. I couldn't help being impressed. He wrote from an officer's training camp, and he sounded busy and ambitious. I answered immediately, and he replied promptly.

From letter to letter my navy boy began to occupy a more special place in my heart. His big, self-confident handwriting demanded a lot of stationery. His letters were soon known to our mailman and to our matron for their bulkiness. At first we both shied away from mentioning any feelings we might have developed for each other, while exchanging our letters more and more frequently.

21

I Changed Gods

How much those letters really meant to me, I recognized after we had corresponded for more than a year. Suddenly the bulky letters stopped. One week, two weeks, three weeks, five weeks passed.

I waited and worried. Would my last letter to him come back someday with that dreaded stamp on it—"*Vermisst*"? I feared to ask for my mail. Eagerly I listened to the navy news during "radio hour" in the evening, especially the U-boat news. Rudy had become a third officer on a U-boat that year, and I knew something about the odds against those men.

The girls had begun to tease me in a sympathetic sort of way, slightly amused that I would worry so much about an unknown man. I denied my concern too loudly and convinced nobody. I began to argue with myself: Was I not being ridiculous? All I knew of him was what he had sent in those bulky letters, plus a picture and a few books. Why should I worry so much about a person whom I had never seen and whom I might never meet, someone who probably cared nothing about me? Or did he care as I did? Why did he write so often, and such long letters? Maybe his boat was lost, or maybe he had just decided to stop writing. No, deep inside I knew that my young officer was not dead. He couldn't be. I had to meet him someday, somewhere. He had become part of my life. I had to believe in him and his future.

When after long weeks his next letter arrived, the matron waited until after dinner to give it to me. I was so skinny, she said she knew I wouldn't have bothered to eat if I had had my twenty-page letter to read!

I tore the parcel-letter open. I struggled to hold back the happy tears, and cared nothing for the teasing remarks of my friends. I had a letter to read; and I read it, hurriedly the first time, carefully and slowly a second and third time.

Rudy had been out for many weeks. *Feindfahrt* (patrol) they called it when the boats cruised the ocean and hunted convoys. His letter was a diary, and he had had no opportunity to mail it for many weeks. Certain things they were forbidden to mention, but whatever was permissible he told. I never cared how many ships they had torpedoed or where his boat had operated; all I wanted to know was about him personally. In one part of his letter he wrote, "When I stand on the bridge during the long hours of my night watch, I look up and see the stars. And I wonder, Marianne, if you are asleep or if you are looking at the same stars. Someday, my dear pen pal, we are going to meet each other, and I cannot wait to see you."

That night I looked at his picture for a long, long time. I knew every line of his face by heart, but I had to study it anew. The picture told me as so often before that he had dark, soft eyes and a very sweet smile. But I had no idea how his voice sounded, how tall he was, or how he walked or laughed.

After I had put the picture down and turned out the lights, I slipped quietly to the window behind my bed and lifted the tight shades a few centimeters. I knew it was against the rules, for every house in the country had to be *verdunkelt* (darkened) at night; any beam of light could betray human dwellings to the bombers, which found their targets anyway with deadly precision night after night. Nobody in his right mind ever lifted a shade before morning dawn—but I had to! I had to see the stars just once in a while, for they had been my friends since earliest childhood. I had watched those wandering lights from my bed in the hayloft many a night and in my heart had talked with them.

Now it was time to talk to the stars again. I had greetings to send! Somewhere a small U-boat sailed on a wide ocean. On it was a young navy officer with brown eyes and a high, intelligent forehead. He might look up at the stars tonight. Would the stars take my greeting to him? Would the stars tell him of the shy love in my heart and the dreams I couldn't help dreaming? Never would I dare to put my feelings into words. Our friendship seemed so precious and frail, words could have destroyed the beauty of it.

Fortune betrayed us. In the spring of 1944 we had begun our third year of writing and we still could only dream and wonder. Would we ever meet? What would we say?

23

I Changed Gods

As total war raged that summer, we were shipped out of the city into the Sudeten mountains. Germany had forgotten what vacation meant; so had we. I was made leader of a group of young girls engaged in hard farm labor. Our male farm hands were somewhere on the fighting fronts. Desperately the women planted and hoed and harvested, learning to do men's work and do it very fast.

Our arms ached as we raked and pulled and lifted from early morning to late afternoon. But we all understood. The farm wife where I worked was sweet and motherly, but she looked haggard and overworked. Each day she slipped some extra food into my apron pocket. I tried to return my appreciation in diligent labor. We became the best of friends.

The extra food, the summer sun, and the large amount of exercise in the fresh air did me many favors. No longer so skinny, I also acquired a healthy tan. My hair, worn in a pageboy style, had grown long over my shoulders, and the sun had bleached it almost blond. War seemed far away in our out-of-the-way camp. No air raids disturbed us as we slept in the quietness of the whispering evergreen woods. Every morning the singing birds awakened us. The morning dew glistened like a thousand diamonds over the pastures when we marched out to the villages for work. When we stood around the flagpole to salute, our voices shouted the pledge with vigor. This was the best summer I had had for years —and Rudy still wrote long letters regularly.

Late one afternoon we checked in from the village, took ice-cold showers, and prepared for supper and evening training. Most of the girls gathered at the athletic field around a girl with an accordion for square dancing and happy chatter. I was late because of duties I carried as a subleader, and I hummed a tune while brushing my hair and creaming my sunburned arms. Then I fell to musing again. I hadn't heard from Rudy for a while and tried hard not to worry. That I couldn't get that boy out of my head was almost disgusting!

It was almost time to leave for the city again. Soon we would have to pack and return to Prague. How much I hated to leave! The summer had been so peaceful. Sure, there had been some friction with that *Führerin*. She was the assistant camp director, and she and I had not been able to get along; but outside of that it had been a dream of a summer. The only thing missing to make everything perfect would have been a visit from— Well, no sense wishing again. Rudy would never be able to come to this remote place. Why should he, anyway?

Starting down the stairway opposite the entrance, I whistled a tune and threw my long hair back, resolutely tossing my head to indicate my determination to stop my silly dreaming.

Suddenly I stopped short. Through the open door stepped a navy officer. His face looked familiar, and suddenly I knew who that man was. I turned in panic and fled to my quarters. There I sat on the edge of my cot and tried to control my beating heart and racing thoughts. I hadn't been so scared in all my life! What if he didn't like my looks? What if— I began to brush my hair again, reset my service pin on my blue house uniform, check myself for invisible spots and blemishes.

Presently I heard my name being called. Summoning all the courage I could find, I walked slowly down the stairs and reported respectfully to the leader in charge. With an amused twinkle in her eyes, she pointed at the navy man and said, "You have a visitor, Marianne. Come and welcome him!"

I looked fully into his smiling face and extended my hand to him. Rudy smiled broadly and said, just a shade too lightly, "Well, here I am, little Hansi!"

I nodded and managed to stammer, "Yes, I can see it—" I could feel myself blushing.

Since my superior had never seen me speechless or self-conscious before, she first looked puzzled, and suddenly laughed a hearty laugh. That seemed to break the tension in the room. Rudy and I also began to laugh, and I finally managed enough self-composure to welcome him and invite him to join the group outside under the big tree, where everybody square danced.

I Changed Gods

Suddenly aware of the sensation Rudy's appearance created, I got my self-confidence back quickly. Proudly I introduced him to my friends, who behind his back gave me little signs of approval or envy. I grinned with delight.

When the supper bell called, Rudy was invited to dine with us. He was seated beside the camp director, a woman of high leadership rank and strict manners. I fulfilled my supervising duties, but I couldn't stop my heart from beating loudly, especially when I stole glances across to Rudy's place. A born charmer, he carried on a gallant conversation with the lady of the camp and at the same time he watched me closely with, it seemed to me, a look of slight amusement. By the end of the meal the *Führerin* of the camp was so favorably impressed by his gentlemanly behavior that she had me signed off from further duty for the evening and the next day, even before I dared ask. Since she had never done such a thing before, this created an even bigger sensation among the girls.

After I had changed into my uniform and returned, we walked slowly out, aware that many eyes watched us. Once outside the campus we turned and walked toward the sunset. Everything around us seemed enchanted, glowing with golden-red and purple. A strange silence seemed to walk between us as Rudy took my hand to help me up the hill. We stood there for a long time watching the fading colors of the evening sky.

We both had felt so close to each other in our letters. Though we had never mentioned this in words, our deep feeling was there between the lines of every page. Now we recognized that the hour of testing of our friendship had come. Both of us feared that a wrong word, an untrue gesture, could break the tender thread. Our friendship now had to face reality. I did not look up as I felt Rudy's eyes searching my profile. Slowly the golden twilight turned into velvety darkness.

"Are you disappointed, little Hansi?" Rudy asked softly.

I shook my head too vigorously and quickly replied: "No—are you, Rudy?"

The Unknown Sailor

He denied it too, but we both knew we were lying. Yes, we both were disappointed. It wasn't that either of us didn't like the other; we were just different from what the other had expected. Dreams are perfect; humans never are. Two and a half years of unreal friendship had suddenly come to an end, and our dreams were irretrievably gone. Were our ties strong enough to face reality and go on?

We determined to give it a try. Sitting on a log, we began to talk. I had so many questions to ask, and I sat and listened as he told me about his life. His voice sounded soft and kind. He acted so young and yet mature at the same time. I watched the stars appear above us, one by one, until the night sky was a diamond-sprinkled dome that surrounded us with new assurance. No, we had not been disappointed after all. Suddenly I knew that I had not, for he really was as I had pictured him all along.

Suddenly I felt, too, that Rudy had received my greetings all through the past years; for the stars talked again to us, and we sat and listened. The stars stepped out of the sky and began to shine within my heart, and I felt that two lights shone in my eyes as we walked hand in hand back to the camp. We both had lost something; our pen pals had left us. But we had found something more precious.

The next day found us happy and at ease with each other. We felt as if we had seen each other many times in the past. I showed him the beautiful countryside, and in high spirits we climbed some hills. Proudly I showed him off to "my" farmers. My motherly friend acted a little shy, but was impressed by all the "brass" and medals. She got busy, and in a short time she had fixed sack lunches for us. She wouldn't listen to my suggestion to let us both help her with her work before we left. We strolled to my little hideouts around the country where I had sat and written to him and dreamed of the time we would meet.

Suddenly Rudy took me into his strong arms to kiss me. I quickly freed myself from his arms and shook my head.

Rudy looked utterly puzzled and distressed. Couldn't he under-

stand? I knew that he had kissed many girls, but he and I—couldn't he understand that it had to be different? For years we had treasured our friendship as something very special. Would it have to go as most war affairs did—passion, kisses, jokes, and fights, leaving a bitter taste in the mouth when it was over? Never! I couldn't fall in love, fall out, and fall in again as some girls do. Maybe I was a dreamer, but I believed someday there would be a great love in my life. I couldn't possibly end this unusual friendship with Rudy in any cheap way, or as an everyday love affair.

Rudy's face was serious as he listened to my attempt to explain how I felt. Then, lifting my chin gently till I looked right into his eyes, he said, "Marianne, have I given you any reason to believe that I would like to use you in any cheap way, or for a fleeting love affair? You have become a part of my life, my great inspiration! I cannot picture my life without you and your letters anymore. You are the type of girl I want to marry someday. Would you?"

Had I heard right? He hadn't by any chance proposed to me? How could he? We had met each other just the day before. I buried my face on his shoulder and as his arms gently enclosed me I looked up. His eyes assured me that my heart had found the great love of my life. Yes, my heart had found its home.

Later, as we lazed in the sun, he talked to me about our future together. Suddenly he said, "My little Hansi, here I am talking to you about our future home, and I am just realizing that I know hardly anything about you. All we do is talk about me and my life; tell me about yourself, your childhood, your family—"

I shrugged my shoulders. What could I tell him? About the little house by the woods, and about my hayloft? Would he understand? He was the only son of a rich home; he had money, security, and the luxuries of life even during the war. Could I tell him of the time when Mother stood at the train station worrying because I might forget God? How could he ever understand? He had a nominal Lutheran background, but religion meant nothing

I sat on a log and the stars appeared above us.

29

to him. He was a Nazi, like me; and he trusted in Hitler and the future of the Reich. No, there was not much to tell.

"Rudy, there is not much to tell about me. I am just a little orphan girl raised in a foster home. As you know, I was selected shortly after the German occupation of my country to be trained as a future youth leader. That training is my life. Everything centers around that goal. I never even thought about marriage because it would interfere with my plans. Wouldn't I let everybody down if I married? I must serve my country someday for all the free education I am getting."

Rudy laughed happily. "Well, Schatzi, why couldn't we do those things together? As soon as the war is over I plan to go into merchant marine, and I will often be gone. You can fulfill your calling and teach. I will not demand all your time."

I smiled, relieved. How simple everything was, how great and how simple! It was time to stop worrying and let go. The great moment of my young life had arrived. I had found my love, and I could trust myself in his hands. Rudy was intelligent, mature, and wise. He had the answers to all my problems, and I was a dumb little girl who couldn't stop worrying.

But now I knew that somebody loved me, and for the first time I dared to love back. War, torpedoes, bombs, death—all seemed impossible as we sat in the flowering pasture with grazing cows on one side and stately evergreens on the other, and above us fluffy white clouds drifting in the bright summer sky over the hazy mountains. Maybe I was dreaming and would wake up to find everything gone and gray, but I would enjoy the dream while it lasted. With new confidence I looked into Rudy's face. Then I looked at the golden band he had put on my finger.

"Rudy, the world you live in seems very different from mine. I do not know if we two will ever be able to fuse our different worlds and backgrounds safely together to build a harmonious partnership. But, Rudy, I am willing to try. As you meet my world, maybe you will learn to understand; and you might learn to love my world as I try to love your world."

30

"Little worry-head, stop philosophizing," laughed Rudy. "Everything will be all right."

Suddenly, like carefree children, we jumped up and ran across the pasture together.

The next day we traveled together to Rudy's home. His parents were polite, though somewhat distant; for our engagement had taken his family and relatives by surprise. But we were too deeply entangled in the task of meeting each other really to care for anything or anybody but ourselves.

How our time flew! We tried to ignore the fact that parting time approached, hoping that by ignoring it we could stop the hour from coming. We had a small engagement party with red roses and fancy wines, which almost scared me in its richness and strangeness. Then Rudy and I sat in a buggy pulled by horses on the way to the train station. The little country train brought us rapidly to Breslau, capital of the province of Silesia. There our two trains were to leave in the afternoon in opposite directions. We arrived before noon, and Rudy took the opportunity to show me his beloved city during our few remaining hours together. For seven years he had gone to school in Breslau, and he knew every corner of that picturesque old place. We ate a few bites in a small cafe, paying not only with money but also with ration stamps provided by his mother. At last the moment came when we had to return to the railroad terminal. For each other's sake we had put on smiles and made lighthearted conversation, trying to disguise how we felt about parting.

Rudy had to leave first. After checking out our suitcases we walked down to the platform and found the train. Rudy's compartment was in the first class, reserved for the "better" element of society even during the days of total war. He reserved his place, stored his suitcase away, and stepped down once more from the train. I had determined to be a brave sweetheart up to the minute of his leaving, and I forced a smile. Trying to cheer me up, Rudy took me into his arms. "Don't be sad, my dear Hansi, we shall see each other soon again. Be my brave little girl

31

meanwhile and wait for me. We shall write each other every day."

That did it! Hiding my face on his shoulder, I burst into uncontrolled sobbing. He pulled out a spotless white handkerchief and began to wipe my face tenderly. I looked up into his kind face and again I felt premonition, that dreadful feeling of danger ahead that I had known when I left my mother to go into Nazi training. Why was I so afraid? I tried to control myself, but it was no use. I cried bitterly, while my heart felt like a stone.

The conductor raised the signal plate and blew the whistle. Rudy kissed me once more and then had to let me go and swing himself onto the already moving train. His face showed the strain of the hour and a deep concern for me. Struggling to calm myself, I finally managed to smile through my tears, but I could not speak. The train gathered speed, and Rudy's waving navy-blue arm with golden stripes and stars grew smaller and dimmer in the distance.

Even after the train had disappeared, I still waved. Then I stopped waving to wipe my tears and began to search for my own train. How I found it and got on it I couldn't remember later.

Would I ever see him again? Would he come back from war? What lay ahead of us? For a few short days I had experienced the warmth of love, the joy of togetherness, the security of having found a home for my heart. All I could think of was Rudy. All I wanted was to be with him. But the trains rolled on into the evening—mine toward the east, his toward the west. Each minute tore us farther apart, while the sun died and the day turned into a long night.

War waited for him; the big city called for me. I cherished the memory of some wonderful days, and the slim golden ring on my finger. As I lifted my hand to feel his ring on my hot face, the golden metal felt cold and strange, just like my lonely heart.

Train wheels sang again, and this is what they sang: "*Ich liebe Dich; auf Wiedersehen. Ich liebe Dich*—[I love you; good-bye. I love you—]"

Beloved sailor, good-bye.

Shattered

I lived from one letter to the next, finding time to answer promptly in spite of our exhausting schedule. After a few weeks, though, I detected a strange note in Rudy's epistles. I asked him what was bothering him, but at first he ignored my questioning.

After three months he told me the truth. His parents, well-to-do people, practical and business-minded, had disapproved of our unusual romance from the beginning. They tried to discourage Rudy from continuing our relationship, and their arguments had the force of parental authority. Rudy's home was very dear to him, and family disharmony proved highly disturbing to his easygoing nature. At last he could hide his problem no longer and told me about it.

I had no choice. I pulled my golden band from my finger, wrapped it in cotton, and sent it without any written message to his parents. Then came the harder part, to write my last letter to him. This is what I wrote:

"Rudy, today I sent my ring back to your mother. There is no question in my mind that I must never stand between you and your parents. I should say, your mother and you. I know how much your home means to you, and I know also that you must never give up your home for my sake.

"I do not know why your mother is against me. I realize that you are wealthy and yours is a very respectable family, while I am only an orphan girl. But Rudy, this part of life I couldn't help; it is not my fault. You know I am trying to find my calling. I might be poor, but I can be proud. I have dedicated my life to the *Führer* and our fatherland, and I shall do my best.

33

I Changed Gods

"Rudy, I never did anything wrong to your mother or you. The only thing she may hold against me is that I have trusted you and that I loved you. May you both forgive me for that!

"I do want to thank you for those wonderful days which we spent together. Somehow I knew from the beginning that it was only a dream and someday there would be a rude awakening. Now the dream has come to an end and it is time to say Good-bye.

"Rudy, you know me well enough; you will understand that there can never be a coming back for us. I have nothing but my pride to protect me, for I am all alone in this world. We must forget each other, and I will do all I can to forget my love for you because my heart has no more right to love. You have been the first and only one I ever trusted enough to love, and it might sound bitter when I say that I wish I had not dared to trust you. It is well said that one doesn't know love until he feels love's anguish. But it seems a lot of ache for a few moments of happiness. Maybe I was never meant to love a man. Maybe I must live only for my work. I don't know if I shall ever dare to love somebody again.

"For your future I wish you only the best and much luck! May you come back unharmed from the war to your family, and may your honorable mother find a girl for you that will make her and you happy!

"For the last time I send you my greeting and my love. Farewell! Maria Anne."

My heart filled with bitter resentment. I could not understand his mother's objection. I did not cry a single tear. The hurt was too deep, the storm in my proud heart too great, to find relief. I busied myself with my duties and studies, lying awake for long hours waiting for the air-raid sirens to sound. I had no more desire to see the stars, so the shades stayed shut tight. Autumn mornings were chilly, and we felt the coal shortage as we shivered in our classrooms. Frosts browned the last purple flower beds as mother earth prepared for a cold winter sleep. My numb heart followed her example.

34

Shattered

It took self-control to march out every morning into biting rain to salute the dripping flag. I hadn't felt warm for days; there was no place to get warm. The rooms were damp and clammy. Our food rations were meager, but it didn't matter to me—I wasn't hungry. One morning I stood before the flagpole saluting when a wave of dizziness overcame me. I forced myself to march back into the house. Then I collapsed.

They put me in a youth hospital in a smaller city. We had excellent treatment, but I was too sick to notice or care. "Contagious jaundice infection" was the diagnosis. The epidemic had raged for weeks, and the hospital was overcrowded. Before long I had lost what I had gained in the summer. I grew pale and thin. I tried not to think too much, for life seemed a strange puzzle with no answers.

Days turned into weeks. My lady doctor ordered new X rays for me, which revealed a stomach ulcer. Sitting down at my bedside, the doctor gave me a motherly smile as she asked: "Little Hansi, is there anything that bothers you—any kind of heartache or worry or problem? You are so listless and withdrawn."

"No." I shook my head defiantly and proudly. I wasn't willing to admit even to myself that anyone could throw me off balance. And Rudy was a closed issue.

A few days later, after my birthday in November, the nurse brought me a forwarded letter. The envelope revealed Rudy's familiar handwriting and the return address showed that he had again been promoted. *"Oberleutnant zur See* [first lieutenant of the navy]," it read. I wondered if he had been called to his new position as second commander on one of the newest U-boats, as he had expected. How proud his parents would be! I wondered if my pride would permit me to open his letter. Yes, I tore the envelope eagerly and read. It was an affectionate birthday message. I read it over and over again, especially the sentence, "Little Hansi, I couldn't let your birthday go by without sending you my warmest wishes—"

No, it was no use. I had to be firm. Quickly I folded his letter

35

up, put it into a new envelope, and mailed it back to him. Rudy didn't know I was so sick, and I didn't want him to know.

Slowly I regained strength and finally one afternoon the doctor promised that I could leave the hospital the next day. I rejoiced. That night, which I thought would be my last one in that house of sickness, the air-raid sirens forced us all out of our beds and into the shelter. Huddled in blankets, we listened indifferently to the droning of the enemy bombers. We always asked the same question: Would the bombers pass over us, or would our own place be their target for the night? We found out all too soon. This was meant for us with love! The bombs exploded nearer and nearer. We knew that the bomb that would hit us would come without singing, so we just sat and waited. By far the hardest attack I had ever experienced, it left us tense and terrified.

At last the siren sounded the departure of the airplanes, and we were allowed to climb back up to our rooms and into our beds. But sleep would not come. We had opened our shades to watch the burning city. Gas and electricity were out, and nurses used flickering candles to take care of some very sick youngsters. The night sky was red from fires and dense with smoke. As I looked out at the dreadful scenes of destruction, I thought of the many lives that had again been snuffed out. Nagging questions again tortured me.

Suddenly I noticed some nurses excitedly run to and fro whispering. I slipped out of bed, still numb and cold from hours in the shelter, and joined the nurses.

What was the problem? Somebody, they said, had detected a dark object on the back ramp of the building, which proved to be *Ein Blindgänger* (a blind walker), a bomb that for some reason had not exploded when it hit the ground. Either it was a time bomb that would explode in a matter of minutes or hours, or it was an ordinary bomb with a short circuit in the releasing device. In any case, the bomb was close enough to demolish the small hospital if it exploded and shatter the windows and sliding doors in our faces.

Shattered

Since any strong vibration, even a loud scream, could explode the bomb, the patients could not be taken down to the shelter nor could the building be evacuated. There was no place to go, for everything around us was fire and ruins.

Noiselessly I stepped up to the back window. In the glow of burning houses across the river I saw the pear-shaped object in its dark outline. Some others stepped up beside me as the news spread quickly through the ward. The nurses had tried to hide the news, fearing panic, but without success. Some patients pulled their blankets over their heads; others cried softly; but everybody tried to avoid commotion and fast movements.

I pressed my hot forehead against the cold window glass. Death and I faced each other again, and my heart started to argue with the grim visitor. I had so many questions to ask, and nobody would answer.

Who was I? Why was I born? Where was I coming from and where was I going? If I had to die that night, what could have been the purpose and reason for my existence? Why must "self-sacrifice" be the highest fulfillment for a human being? Everything seemed shallow and intangible in the face of death. My high ideals and goals seemed powerless to comfort. I imagined that the Grim Reaper sat out there on top of that metal object and grinned into my bewildered eyes.

My heart cried out for more understanding and more insight; but smoke covered the fading stars, and the dawn had to fight its way through clouds of dust and charred ruins. Everything within and around me seemed vague and empty. We just stood motionless and waited.

As soon as it was light enough, a noiseless crew appeared. Obviously the men were prisoners, as an armed guard marched behind them. Since we young people had never heard about concentration camps and political prisoners, we had no idea who those sad, gray figures were. They moved in cautiously, like cats, toward the bomb and examined it long and carefully. Then one man bent over while others handed him some tools. Ever so precisely he began to take the detonator apart. At last he stopped, nodded, got up from his knees, and wiped his forehead. The bomb was *entschärft* (de-sharpened), and the prisoners carried the different parts away.

Normal life resumed in the ward, and a nurse ordered me back to bed. With a last look out the window, I turned away. I had seen the Grim Reaper walk out of the yard. Once again he had turned his back on me as he returned to the smoldering city to find more prey among the ruins. Farewell, grim neighbor. We shall meet again!

After a few days, as soon as a certain amount of order had been established and trains were running again, I was dismissed. I reported back to school at once in spite of my doctor's recommendation to take a vacation and recover my full health. Where should I go to find rest? The little house in the woods was so far away, and I hadn't heard from Mother for a long time. Mail was delayed. Too many trains and tracks were being destroyed. Rudy was not mine anymore, and I had no right to go to his comfortable home in eastern Germany. Possibly his parents and sister were not even there anymore. I had heard rumors that the Russians had already broken through into Silesia and the refugees had fled through winter storms to get away.

No, I had nowhere to go, and I was eager to work again. My staff leader received me gladly, for every willing hand was needed to meet the emergencies of total war. Week after week we struggled and toiled, often sharing our small food rations with refugees and wounded soldiers who seemed more hungry than we. My stomach gave me terrible pains. Ulcers demanded certain kinds of food, but who cared about such trivialities?

One day in March, 1945, we got orders from headquarters to leave Prague immediately and go home. Perplexed, I reported to my leader in charge and asked for permission to stay. First of all, I had no place to go, and besides, there was still so much work to do. How could we all leave?

My *Führerin* shook her head firmly: "No, Marianne, orders

are orders. The city is no longer safe for you girls. The Russians are approaching fast!

I shook my head innocently. "Why worry about that? Our armies will drive the enemies back in a short time." Had not Adolf Hitler spoken the day before over the radio and promised that victory would come soon? With the new miracle weapons our German scientists were getting ready, Germany would be able to rout our enemies within days. The end of the war was in sight. Couldn't I stay?

"My girl, you must leave today," she replied. "Don't you have any relatives?"

"Yes. My sister in Reichenberg. I don't know her very well because we did not meet each other until a few years ago. Her husband fell on the battlefield in Russia. She was left with three children. Maybe I could stay with her for a few weeks until I come back to school."

My superior wrote an emergency ticket for the train and I left wondering about the strange expression on her face as I bade her *"Auf Wiedersehen."*

The trip was long and often interrupted, but I finally arrived at my sister's place. Weeks later I learned that the Russians had entered Prague a few hours after I left. My train must have been one of the last to pull out of the terminal before the Russians marched in. Rumors about a terrible *Blutbad* (blood bath) that followed made me shudder. Czech nationalists killed hundreds of Nazis who had not been able to leave on time. Death had missed me again. Why? Most likely the woman who had made me leave saved my life, but lost hers.

It was a balmy day in May when Admiral Doenitz, Rudy's commander, spoke over the air. We sat before my sister's radio and listened intently. Doenitz had, by Hitler's last will, taken the reigns of our leaderless nation to carry on. In a matter of hours, even though it was not officially announced, the whole country knew and whispered from door to door that Hitler and his mistress Eva Braun had committed suicide!

I Changed Gods

We were stunned. Why would Hitler do such a ghastly thing? Hadn't he promised to lead us to victory? Still, I didn't question Hitler's decision. I couldn't understand, but I trusted that our hero knew what was best for the nation and in that mysterious act of "self-sacrifice" had shown a way for us. I could not entertain the thought that Hitler, my god and idol, could have used a coward's way out of a predicament of his own making.

Two days later the Russians marched into Reichenberg. I stared into those strange faces as the soldiers tramped and rolled in past my sister's house toward the city center. I stood behind the window curtains and watched, numb with fright and unbelief, and waited! Yes, I knew that Hitler was dead—but I still trusted and believed him. I knew that Hitler's promises would be fulfilled; it was only a matter of time!

I do not know how I lived through the next few weeks. Slowly it began to dawn on me that I had believed a big lie. Hitler's golden image within my heart began to crumble—then it fell. My life seemed shattered, my mind stupefied. I felt as if I were falling into a bottomless pit.

Thousands, millions, felt as I felt—and many could not take it. They followed Hitler to the last and many like him, died by suicide. Several Nazi party leaders in Reichenberg chose that way out. Parents poisoned their children and died together with them. The occupying army didn't care. In many cases it saved their bullets, which they generously used anyway.

The days seemed to get darker as time dragged on. I felt that I had come to the end of the road, always hungry, always hiding from lewd soldiers. But human beings can bear more than they think they can, as I found out soon.

One morning I was required to report at a Communist labor center, and soon I found myself perched high on an open truck with many other girls and women. We were swiftly transported across the German-Czech line deep into the interior of Bohemia.

By late afternoon we arrived at a huge farm, Communist style. The place had several buildings including large barns. Surround-

40

ing the farm was a high stone wall with two gates. It was evident that the estate must have been the manorial domain of a rich Czech proprietor, recently confiscated.

The new manager and overseers, we soon discovered, had been picked from the ranks of the farmhands who had served the land-owner. These new bosses had little aptitude for their positions but attempted to compensate with shouting and arbitrary orders.

Dazed from hunger, we climbed off the vehicle and faced a brute of a man, our new overseer. He shouted some commands, and I understood that we were supposed to climb up a shaky ladder that led into a kind of attic in the barn. There we found a few old cots, and some fresh straw spread on the floor—our new sleeping quarters!

In my heart raged a storm of hate. Realizing how easily they had tricked me into a labor camp, I hated myself for having been so gullible. I looked around. There was no chance of escape; we were far from German territory. We were marked by a white band on the left sleeve as "Germans." The walls were high, and the whole place swarmed with hostile, suspicious people. We had no choice; we might as well submit quietly.

The next morning, after a meager breakfast, we were ordered at sunrise into the fields. The new regime demanded production, and our overseer was more than eager to put on a good show. He rushed us mercilessly from the first minute.

We worked doggedly. My suppressed fury speeded my work. As the sun rose, the heat became unbearable; we had no water. Putting my rake down, I crossed the field and faced the sullen overseer. "The girls need water or they will not be able to work very well," I said in Czech. "We are dizzy, and some will faint." His eyes and mine met for some seconds.

I thought he was getting ready to strike me, but instead he forced a sly smile on his face and replied, "Very well, you girls shall have some water, just because you asked for it, Manjo (Czech for Mary). I see that you are a fast worker, Manjo. I hope you will become my helper in many ways!"

41

Shattered

I turned wordlessly and walked back to my work, thinking, "Who does he think I am? His 'helper,' ha!"

"Control yourself, girl; control yourself," I murmured as I dug my nails into my clenched fists. I had to learn to be quiet or it would make things worse, for me and the others.

We got drinking water that first day; but there were other days when the man's ugly mood controlled him, and we had to work without water. Girls fainted, women screamed, and the frustrated overseer used his fists to urge us on. But he never bothered me. Somehow he treated me with a reluctant respect and left me alone. He knew that the girls had made me their spokesman, and my influence on them could be felt as we reached our work quota. I had the girls organized so that two more able workers would take a weak or unskilled girl in the middle. As soon as a girl lagged behind, we faster workers stepped in and helped her so she could catch up. This way we protected each other from beatings most of the time.

In spite of our efforts, our group diminished in size. Nobody bothered to discuss it. Life had become a nightmare of hunger, thirst, hard work, and fear.

The days would have been bearable, but the nights! A few days after we arrived, the soldiers stationed in the next village found out about our German girl group. That night they broke into our sleeping quarters, led in by our grinning overseer. I was one of the few who got away unmolested.

We knew our chances for undisturbed sleep were slim from then on. The soldiers would be back and bring their comrades along to join the hunt. I had vowed in my heart that I would rather die than surrender to my enemies. Death seemed close indeed. Nothing kept me going but my pride, hatred, and stubbornness. I determined that I would fight and scratch like a wildcat till they shot me.

But so far I had never needed to fight to protect myself. It seemed as if an unseen power was taking care of me. The other girls had noticed this, and asked, "Manjo, what kind of good-luck

*"The girls need water," I told
the overseer, "or some will faint."*

charm do you have? Nothing happens to you. The overseer is leaving you alone, and the soldiers didn't bother you. You never faint in the fields."

"*Unsinn* [nonsense]," I replied. "You know better than to be superstitious. Good-luck charms are old women's stuff. There is nothing special about me."

But deep inside, I began to wonder. It was the same feeling Rudy had told me about once when he survived so many close calls. Something really seemed to protect me, but what? The religious convictions of my childhood had been so thoroughly brainwashed out of me that it did not occur to me that God might have been my Defender. The whole situation seemed so incomprehensible, but it was real.

On the other hand, I didn't know how long my luck would last, and I was not eager to take any chances. After that first visit of the soldiers I began to look around with a purpose. We knew they would be back again, and we knew that nobody would bother to stop them. The overseer seemed pleased that he could be of service to his Russian friends. The other girls and women depended on me for advice and help, so I had to find a solution.

The first thing to do was to find a hiding place. But where? We had to stay within the court because the gates were locked at night, and the Russians enforced a merciless curfew. Czechs, Slovenians, and Germans alike were subject to it.

Then I found it. At the far end of the large farmyard stood an old barn half filled with straw and hay. The building could be entered by a small side door whenever the large doors were closed at night. We tried it. Late every evening when we could hear the overseer snoring, we noiselessly climbed down our old chicken ladder, sneaked across the courtyard one by one, and slipped cautiously through the small door into the straw. We dug individual "caves" into the fresh straw, and it seemed more comfortable than in our former sleeping quarters. Each night the entire group migrated to this place, where we enjoyed better rest and greater security.

44

Shattered

With the coming of summer heat, tensions seemed to mount, and tempers grew short. We thought of little else than our need for more food and rest. We stopped counting days. We had no calendar. We staggered through the days with scarcely a thought for the morrow, because all was hopeless.

One day in July everything went wrong. We were not permitted to take water out, and the heat had become sultry and oppressive. Thunderclouds threatened the ripening grain and made the overseer nervous. Before our eyes he hit a young mother who had stopped raking to still her fussing child. I could hardly bear watching it without retaliation. We listened to the cries of mother and child. Then we quarreled among ourselves, and some girls cried.

Sunburned and exhausted, we finally dragged ourselves back to our quarters where, after a few bites of poor food, we climbed the ladder to the straw. Desperately I fought off sleep after we retired, because I knew that I must awaken the girls for our excursion to the barn. It was especially important that night, for new Russian troops had been coming in that afternoon, and some soldiers had seen us as we worked in a field beside the country road. Some soldiers had even stopped to inquire of the overseer. These soldiers would know before evening where we could be found. I couldn't afford to go to sleep; I had to get us all out in time.

As I dozed, my mind began to wander. I could hardly believe that it had been just a year since I had taken part in that summer aid program in the Sudeten mountains. Yes, and it would soon be a year from the time when Rudy had come to that remote spot and we had run across the flowery pasture under smiling sunshine and fluffy white clouds. I could hear myself saying to him, "Rudy, tell me that I am not just dreaming. Oh, Rudy!"

How hard I had tried not to think of him during the past few months. What had become of him? Was he still alive? Maybe his U-boat had gone under as so many had shortly before the end of the war. If his boat had come back, where was he? Maybe in

45

a prison camp? How had he taken it that Germany had lost the war? He had been such an optimistic and enthusiastic Nazi. Neither of us had even considered the possibility of a German defeat. Maybe he had committed suicide like some other officers. As I saw it, suicide seemed the most noble way out of the whole mess, and I had considered it several times, especially since I had been pressed into this labor camp. But how could a person do it? I had no gun or fast-acting poison. Besides, was it really a noble way out? Mother would say that it would be an escape for cowards.

What about Mother? Most likely she was dead. I hadn't seen her for five years. Frail little woman, how much chance would she have had in these last months of starvation and suffering? Father was gone for sure. He had depended upon medicine and doctor's care from day to day. It was easier to picture those I loved as being dead. Better this than to think Mother might have to go through days like mine.

Maybe Rudy had been caught by the Russians. No, I wanted him to be dead too; not hungry as I was and hunted like a defenseless animal. It seemed so desirable to be dead!

Quietly I got up and awakened the girls. Accustomed by then to climb noiselessly down the wobbly ladder, we made our way quickly over to the barn. As I reached out both hands to open the squeaky side door, something told me not to go in. Or was it a voice? Surprised, I turned around. Behind me stood the silent group of girls huddled together in fright.

I shook my head in disgust. "Manjo," I thought, "you are getting crazy and you are beginning to hear ghosts."

Again I stepped forward to enter and a second time something seemed to say within me, "Don't go in that barn tonight."

In an instant I had decided. My deep urge was clear and strong, and while I could not understand who or what was warning me, I knew I felt the same way as when I had left Mother, and when I had said good-bye to Rudy. I knew that I had to obey that voice.

I whispered to the waiting girls, "I won't go in tonight."

"Why not, Manjo? We are so tired and want to go back to sleep. Look! we have been safe in that barn for many nights!" The girls began to whisper and get noisy.

"Hush," I said firmly. "You all may go in—I will not stop you. It's only that I don't want to go in myself, that's all."

The girls were undecided, but then one girl said, "Oh, no. If Manjo doesn't go into the barn tonight, I will not go in either. She usually knows what she is doing."

Nobody wanted to enter that barn. But, what to do next? That same inner urge seemed to tell me what to do next. "We must leave these premises tonight," I whispered, and began to walk quietly toward the locked east gate. The girls followed me. One of my closest friends among the group hurried close to my side and whispered in fright, "Hansi, I hope you know what you are doing! Do you realize what a chance we are taking? If we are found outside the walls, we will be shot without warning. You know how the Russians are enforcing the curfew. Nobody is allowed out after 9:30, not even the Czech people!"

"Yes, Lilo, I know. But somehow I just feel we must get out of here for tonight. I don't know how to explain it. Please don't ask any more questions, for we must hurry."

I had learned how to open the gate some days before through a kind Czech woman who had secretly befriended me. Quickly I had the mechanism released, and through the slightly open gate the frightened girls slipped out into the fields. As soon as I had closed the gate, I followed the group. The night was still, and the moon and stars seemed cruel in their brightness, for they betrayed our moving forms. Close to the woods we found a field where we had harvested alfalfa a few days before. The hay had been stacked on high wooden contraptions to dry out. I suggested that the girls crawl under those haystacks for protection and a little sleep. The girls obeyed without delay. My girl friend and I also squeezed under one of the stacks and tried to make ourselves comfortable. But sleep stayed away that night. Danger seemed to lurk around every corner, and we were tense and apprehensive. The frogs croaked loudly in a nearby pond. Other night noises from the woods sounded strange and forbidding. We heard the barking of dogs, now closer, now fading into the distance again, as we sat with cramped muscles and waited.

At last the stars began to pale till we could see signs of day in the east. Dawn was our salvation, because we knew that every Russian soldier had to return by morning light, and their army discipline was very strict. They would have left by the time we had stolen our way back to our sleeping quarters at the labor camp.

We managed to get back in time without being detected by the overseer. After a short while he blew the whistle and we all "got up" and formed our routine line for report and breakfast.

With more disgust than usual I noticed the breakfast menu—soup, consisting mainly of water and salt and some potatoes, besides some crusts of dry bread. I couldn't help wondering if the cook let the bread mold systematically before he portioned it out to us in stingy rations. How could any kitchen produce so much spoiled bread at all times without deliberate planning?

Well, it really didn't matter; we were hungry enough to devour anything edible. As the line began to move, I eagerly awaited my turn because my stomach hurt so much when I was hungry. Suddenly I felt a gentle nudge in my ribs. Looking up, I saw the kind face of that Czech woman who had been our secret friend.

"*Děvčatko* [little girl]," she whispered while trying to appear inconspicuous. "I got to tell you something!"

"*Ano* [yes]?" I mumbled.

"The Russians were here last night!"

I nodded, unimpressed. Her words were really no news at all.

"Listen, Manjo. It was really very bad!" She pointed toward the kitchen. "One of those women over there betrayed you last night. She told those drunken soldiers where you had been hiding. Oh, those sons of the devil." She crossed herself fearfully. "They were so mad because they couldn't find you and made so much

48

commotion. Do you know what they did? Those *hloupy rucky* [stupid Russian] beasts got into the barn where you have been sleeping and looked through the straw. When they were not able to find you, they used their bayonets to jab through the straw, swearing and shouting, 'Those German pigs will squeak when we stab them!'

"Though they hunted for you the whole night," she continued, "they couldn't find you anywhere. In the name of our holy saint, where did you hide? I shall burn a candle to our Holy Madonna next Sunday for protecting you. Oh, you poor *Nemci* [Germans], *jsem rad* [I am glad] that you are not hurt."

As she hurried off, I stammered a soft *Dekuji* (thank-you) after her.

So it was known that we had been hiding in the barn! But who had told me not to go in last night? It would have cost our lives if the trigger-happy soldiers had found us.

I passed the news to the girls around me, and their whispering went like the morning wind down the line on both sides of me. Carefully, slowly, in order not to arouse our overseer's suspicion, the girls crowded around me and implored, "Manjo, how did you know? Manjo, who told you that we shouldn't sleep in that barn last night? Manjo, what charm do you use?"

I shrugged. "I don't know, girls; I really don't know. It was just—well, I can't explain it!"

The line moved quickly on because the overseer yelled impatiently. Receiving my soup, I drank it hurriedly. I tried to bring order into my muddled brain while I chewed my hard crust of *chleb* (bread), but it was no use. Everything seemed hazy, and I couldn't command my thinking into the right direction. Something had gone wrong with me. My memory did not work!

I tried to reach back into my thoughts, to tie past and present together, but it was no use. I tried to remember some basic things like home or Mother or Rudy, and couldn't. Worst of all, those figures suddenly lacked names. No, it was not possible. I couldn't have forgotten Mother's name. Oh, what was Mother's name?

I Changed Gods

Obviously, I was going crazy. Maybe soon my aching head would burst, and I would do something irrational and go hysterical. I knew what that would mean. If I cracked up as others I had known—the solution was simple: one or two bullets.

No, I had to get away from my persecutors while I could still make decisions. I wouldn't surrender and give that ugly overseer the devilish satisfaction that he had broken me—that he had won! No, I would fight, escape, leave, walk out. If they killed me, OK—at least it wasn't a surrender!

As soon as we had arrived at our assigned place of work, I announced my departure to the girls around me. Some wanted to go with me, and I grimly nodded my agreement.

We looked at the direction of wind and sun; then when the overseer had left our field, we deliberately walked away. Woods are plentiful in Bohemia, and we hurried toward the nearest one. As soon as we had reached the dark coolness of the dense evergreens, we moved steadily northward, listening anxiously for any threatening noises.

Our overseer must have felt very sure of himself. He knew how deep we were in Czech territory. He knew also that Russian soldiers combed the area for escaped prisoners everywhere. He knew we would be caught sooner or later and be brought back.

I do not know how long we walked and hid and struggled through woods and fields, but we finally reached the Sudeten territory, and at last I arrived at my sister's.

My sister Grittli asked few questions after she had cautiously opened the door to answer my knocking. She quietly led me upstairs where I could hide and sleep undisturbed. I fell upon the mattress, and Grittli removed my shoes. Her motherly hand put a blanket over me, and while I sank into deep sleep I mumbled into the pillow, "Everything is shattered, Sis, all broken up. But things will be all right after I wake up. It's just a bad dream I am having."

Morning Dawn

CHAPTER 5

After long hours of sleep, I woke up and tried to collect my thoughts. Oh, yes, I was at my sister's place and in a bed upstairs in an attic room.

Quickly I got up. At least, I tried to do so. But my body was sore, and my feet ached so badly that I hobbled painfully out of the room and down the stairs.

My sister, who had tried to keep her three little girls quiet all those long daylight hours that I might sleep, had some soup ready. Brave little woman! How she managed to keep things going was beyond my understanding. Somehow she managed most of the time to find a bit of flour somewhere, a loaf of bread, a cabbage head, some lettuce from her small garden to feed her hungry children. Even the baby girl, Uta, my favorite niece and our pride and joy, seemed to do fine. She eagerly ran into my outstretched arms, gurgling happily with baby talk.

There was no safety for me at my sister's, and we talked softly so as not to alarm the children. My persecutors would find me; it would be just a matter of time. My next term in a labor camp would be farther east—much farther east! Russia is big! We decided that I would stay at my sister's place for a few days until I had regained my strength, then try to decide what to do next.

I hadn't had so much sleep in months. Willingly my sister shared her meager supply of food with me. Slowly I felt more like myself again. If only my mental haziness would go away! It made me feel that I was my own prisoner. I was careful not to mention it to my sister, though. Maybe she would think I was crazy. Maybe I was!

Soon I had to make another decision. Not far from us lived a prosperous Czech family who had been friendly toward our family for a long time. The son of the family belonged to the National Guard. When he found out that I had returned to my sister's place, he visited us regularly, assuring us of his good intentions and even bringing us small amounts of bread and potatoes. I treated him politely, but laughed at my sister's suggestion that Vladislav was courting me.

I stopped laughing when our young neighbor came to see me one day and asked gravely if he might talk to me. I nodded politely, and we went for a walk. It was safe to leave the house with him beside me because his position protected me even though I wore my white armband. Vladislav, after stuttering for a while, announced that he had just received orders to bring me to the labor office in the city. I was horrified. Would he really do it?

He hesitated, then continued. "Manjo, there is not a thing you can do about it. Even if you hide, the militia will find you by and by. But," and his round, simple face blushed as he continued, "there is one way out for you, and that is to marry a Czech man. It would change your status and you would be considered a free citizen of the Czech Republic. Well, and—and—since I feel real love in my heart for you, and since I am well able to start my own *domečku* [little home] for both of us, will you consider it?"

I looked into his red, sweaty face. Was Vladi aware of what he was doing? Other Czech men had dared to marry German girls within the last few months, and many more German girls were trying to make such contacts as an easy way out of a desperate situation. But with my young neighbor it was different! As a *národny* (national Czech) his marriage with a German girl could endanger his future career.

I shook my head. "No, Vladi, that is not good for you and your future. I thank you for your willingness to save me from labor camp, but I cannot accept the offer!"

The young man was not easily convinced. He urged, pleaded,

and threatened. After all, he had the power to take me to the officials! My mind raced. I had to have time to think.

Meekly I asked him if he would give me time to think it over. The proposal had come as a surprise to me, and I had to think about it first and ask my sister for advice.

Vladi nodded happily and smiled, relieved, and walked me back to my sister's home. Before I slipped through the door, he assured me again that not only my problems but my sister's would be over as soon as I gave my Yes. Vladi would bring food for the children, and clothing, shoes—I nodded a friendly good night and went inside.

I could never marry that Czech man. I had not a spark of love for him in my heart, and I was prejudiced enough toward the Czechs as a whole that I would never join them. But I had no choice but to stall him. It was tempting to say Yes and give up struggling, but I just couldn't do it. If nothing else, it would not be fair to him. I could not make him happy and I didn't want to either!

In two days he would return from a patrol trip, so I lost no time! Hastily I packed some clothing in a knapsack and my sister helped me to sew my few valuable possessions into the lining of my overcoat. The only document I took with me was my Catholic birth certificate. All my other important papers I laid in an air-tight metal box and buried it in the backyard during the night. My report cards, diplomas, and other records were Nazi papers, signed and sealed with different stamps bearing the Nazi eagle and swastika. I didn't dare carry them on my flight from home.

Flight? Yes, I had to flee; but where? We knew that the "left-overs" of Germany had been divided. Western Germany lay far to the west of us. Now Eastern Germany had become a Communist republic, heavily occupied by Russian troops. Western Germany was occupied by the Allies, mainly Americans. Rumor had it that the American zone of Germany was a good place to live, that the Americans were friendly. There was a ration card system, and people could buy food. Not much, of course, but enough to keep alive. The American soldiers, it was said, did not force their attentions on women; enough girls liked to be *Solda-ten-Liebchen* (soldiers' sweethearts) so that the Americans left other people alone. This sounded too good to be true, and nobody knew anything for sure; but just in case that those marvelous reports were true I would try to go there. If I made it and found things otherwise, I wouldn't have lost anything.

One night later I left for Western Germany. I was not alone. One of my girl friends wanted to join me, and I didn't have the heart to turn her down. Her parents had been taken to a labor camp, and she was alone and helpless. My sister's children had already gone to sleep when I bent sadly over Uta's small baby bed. I loved that child! Would I ever see her again? Would I ever see anybody again? My sister put a crust of bread into my knapsack and a few dried blueberries. I knew she had taken them from her own children.

We did not say much as I stepped out the back door. What was there to say? I looked once more over to Vladi's house. Everything was dark. I wondered how he would feel when he returned the next day and found the bird flown. Would he become a real German-hater? I knew I was betraying his trust. Would he ever understand that I was doing the best for both of us? "Good-bye, Vladi. Good luck to you, and thanks for your kindness. May you forgive me that I chose freedom rather than a life of ease!"

We soon reached the borderline between Czechoslovakia and East Germany. Both parts were occupied by Russian troops and governed by Communists. Therefore the boundary was not carefully guarded, and we got across it unmolested.

We took off our white bands, which had marked us for so long as outcasts, for East Germany did not require them. Then with new hope we began our long tramp through East Germany. Unfortunately the weather seemed to turn against us and all the other refugees who milled around all over the country. It rained for hours, for days, for weeks. We moved on as in a nightmare with drenched clothing clinging to our bodies until a merciful sun shone for a few hours and dried us a little. Our hungry stomachs woke us up at night while we tried to sleep in the woods or hide in ditches.

There were evenings when I was so exhausted and racked by pains from my ulcered stomach that I was tempted to quit. For food we had only a few herbs from the woods, wild berries, and roots. Did it make any sense to keep going? Oh, yes, there was Micherle, the girl that had trusted her life into my hands when she had joined me in my long journey. If nothing else, I had to keep going for her sake.

At night, whenever we were lucky enough to find a fairly dry shelter to sleep under, we would dream of food—rich, appetizing, warm, tantalizing food. We eagerly reached for it only to wake up empty and cold. We talked about food, tried to remember how certain things tasted. We did not long for fancy stuff; just a bowl of soup, a good piece of bread, fresh boiled potatoes. But there was nobody to share with us—too many refugees on the roads. The farmers and villagers kept their homes locked, the barns barred, the orchards and fields guarded by dogs and traps.

But my greatest trial was my befuddled mind! My memory had not returned after many days, and I tormented myself for hours trying to force my brain to remember. I was obsessed with the search for my mother's name, but could not find it regardless of how hard I tried.

One ray of light shone, one consolation, one hope. In the darkest hours of discouragement and despair, while cold, sleepless, and bent over with pain, I was able to close my eyes and think of Mother. I didn't know her name; I couldn't remember so many incidents of my childhood, but I still could visualize her as a person. Whenever my heart called for her, she seemed to be there; and my vision of her was always, of all things, in the frame of sunset worship!

There she sat at the window looking out toward the crimson evening sky or the dark clouds that towered above the hills. Her blue eyes would get a faraway look, then she would start to sing.

Her voice was not fancy or full, but silvery like a child's voice. She would run out of breath before the end of the phrase was reached, because her heart was not strong and she was short of breath. She loved *"Näher mein Gott zu Dir* [Nearer My God to Thee]" and *"Oh, bleibe Herr, der Abend bricht herein* [Abide With Me]," and we all joined in. After the singing, Father would reach for the family Bible and read a psalm. It had to be a psalm for sunset worship on Friday and Sabbath. I still could picture the way he sat in his chair at worship time and gravely recited the words of the Scriptures.

After Father's reading we all knelt in prayer on the fresh-scrubbed wooden floor. After we had finished praying we children had to shake our parents' hands and respectfully wish them God's blessings. Yes, Mother's worship hours stayed with me when nothing else did. Only the memory of those precious minutes kept me going. I could still remember the peace that had settled in my heart during such times, and my heart longed for it again. Mother's peace! Mother—I thank you! Your faithfulness in little things saved my life. You were so careful to be ready by sunset to welcome the Sabbath. Oh, that every Christian mother would take time for family worship and be ready for the Lord's day! There would be so much peace!

After crossing the larger part of Thuringia, we arrived in the last village before *Niemandsland* (no-man's-land), a strip of land several kilometers wide between East and West Germany. We learned that Communist border guards patrolled the area, and no one was allowed within that zone. The soldiers had orders to shoot at any moving object. Other refugees who milled about the village told us this.

It did not seem fair that we had struggled, hungry and wet, through all those weeks only to be stopped by an uncrossable strip of land. I had to find a way, but how? Refugees I talked to sounded frustrated and defeated; it was foolishness to take a chance. Many had done so and been killed or imprisoned.

Dusk had settled over the village, and as the dripping fog

rolled in from the river we shivered in our wet clothing. Clouds promised another heavy rain. Some windows lighted up behind drawn shades, suggesting warmth and a sense of belonging. How would it feel to sit near a big stone hearth and get warmed up again—warmed through and through?

On a sudden impulse, I walked up to a house and knocked! A weatherbeaten sign told us that it had been a *Gasthaus* (guesthouse) in its better days, but naturally it was closed, for the *Gastwirt* (innkeeper) had nothing to offer anymore. Yes, I knew it was senseless to knock, and my girl friend's round eyes stared at me in surprise. Had I forgotten that doors did not open to people like us? People didn't bother anymore even to look at the homeless, foodless, shelterless refugees who filled the roads. They didn't even bother to answer their knocking. But I knocked again, loud and eager, with determination.

Unexpectedly the door opened, and I looked into the kind eyes of an elderly man. "What do you want?" he asked hesitatingly.

"Sir," I stammered, "we are so cold and soaked by the rain, we wondered if we could sit for a while beside your hearth to get dry?"

Of course he wouldn't let us in; why should he? Two strange girls with their clothes dripping, the water squeezing in the old torn shoes—he would slam the door in our faces, and we would walk sadly into the night again.

"Well, come on in," said the man, after looking us over from our heads to our toes. "You poor girls!"

Had I heard right? The man was inviting us in?

With a humble *Danke* (thank-you) we stepped into the house, took off our shoes so we would not dirty the floor, and sat down by the hearth to dry our clothing. Oh, how good it felt to be warm! If we didn't disturb anyone, maybe we could sit by the hearth until the people retired?

After a while the man came toward us with two steaming bowls of soup in his hands. Smiling, he asked us whether we wanted to eat some soup! Our hands trembled as we reached out for the bowls. We thanked the kind man over and over again.

Gratefully we handed back the empty bowls and spoons and sat quietly, waiting for the word that would send us out again into the stormy night. I felt a strong desire to talk to that friendly man about our plans to cross the border into the West. But it was not wise to trust anybody; to open my heart to a stranger might prove disastrous. Still this man had been so kind. Would he turn around and betray us if we asked for advice?

Time ticked away at the old cuckoo clock, and I knew I had to hurry. I threw my hair back over my shoulders with a determined head shake and said, "Sir, may I ask you a question?"

The man nodded.

"I don't have to tell you that we are refugees. We left my homeland, Czechoslovakia, weeks ago. We came west to cross the border, but we did not know about this no-man's-land. Sir, we've got to get across it, but we don't know how. Do you have a map of this area so we could find a way? We would like to cross tonight."

The man began to laugh. No, not malicious—it sounded like a friendly, amused laugh. But why would a man laugh under such circumstances?

"You naïve little things!" he said. "You sound like a dog barking at the moon. How can you think of crossing the countryside with only a map? No, no, girls! Soldiers are out there day and night to catch you. You couldn't possibly make it."

"But, sir," I pleaded, "isn't there any way at all? I've got to leave, because I escaped from a labor camp. If I stay here they will find me and put me back into one of those horrid camps."

"Yes," he finally answered, "there is one pass yet where Germans are going across, but the way is very hard to find. Only a guide can lead you through, and"—his voice became a whisper—"there is such a guide in the village. It's the ferryman down at the river. If you can pay him enough he may take you, but he is asking a lot. He wants watches, jewelry—"

I interrupted him excitedly. "Sir, we have a few things hidden in the lining of our clothing. Maybe it will be enough to please him. At least we can try. Oh, thank you, sir, for being so kind and open toward us. I do not know how I ever can repay you, but let me assure you of our deepest appreciation!"

The man nodded, rose from his chair, and said simply, "You girls may sleep in our house tonight. Not even a dog should be out on a night like this, and you girls look as if you need some rest. Tomorrow you can see the ferryman."

He led us upstairs to a room with two beds. The cover on each bed was a bulging *Federbett* (feather bed), and there were soft pillows. He bade us good night and left.

We looked at each other dumbfounded. We must be dreaming! People like that man didn't really exist! The beds felt real, and though the raindrops drummed on the small window, no rain was hitting us.

Before we retired, we ripped certain parts of our clothing open and laid our treasures out on a little pile. It wasn't a fortune, but the things seemed valuable enough to make a try the next morning. The only thing I hated to lose was a silver bracelet Rudy had sent me. A piece of my heart went along with it. Another thing I had treasured was my colorful silken scarf. The scarf made a bright little bundle after we had tied our valuables in it. Then we eagerly slipped under the soft feather covers. We felt guilty to be sleeping so comfortably, for we knew how many of our fellow refugees were out in the rain.

During the night I awakened several times with a feeling of dread. "Maybe we're in a trap," I thought. "When will somebody come in and order us out? Surely we cannot sleep a whole night in a soft, warm bed!"

Nobody came to chase us out. When morning came, I awakened Micherle because we had to go and find the ferryman. She was not too happy about rising early; who knew when we might sleep in a real bed again?

Careful not to disturb our kind host's family, we tiptoed out of the house and stepped into a dull gray morning. For the first time in days our clothing was dry, and we felt warm and rested. In our hearts we felt a new hope. The happenings of the last evening seemed like a good omen.

Arrived at the river, we found it dirty with yellow-brown mud, and swiftly flowing as a result of continuing rain. We waited at the wharf, and I felt a pang of fear when the ferry appeared. What if the man said No? What if he asked for more pay? We had nothing more to give!

With a forced cheery, "Good morning," we stepped on the raft and paid our fee. The man steered quietly across, gazing silently into the water. We were the only passengers, and as we reached the middle of the river I took a deep breath and began my speech.

"Sir," I said, "somebody has told us that you are a guide who will take refugees across the border if the pay is equal to the chance you are taking. Now, sir"—I talked in haste so he would not interrupt until I had finished—"I do not know whether our valuable things we brought with us will be enough, but look and see." Hastily I untied my bundle and laid it at his feet.

"No. I don't do such things. You know that the Russians would shoot me if they caught me doing that!"

I nodded emphatically. "Yes, I know, but look. We *must* get across. Believe me, we are not spies. We have come from Czechoslovakia and have walked a long, long way. Please help us! I escaped from a labor camp, so I ran away and my girl friend with me. Is it not enough that we offer you? Look at it, sir. It's all we have to give, friend. We hold nothing back. Won't you take us?"

He stared at my bundle and remained silent for what seemed a long time. At last he nodded his unkempt head and said, "Ja, girls, I will take you tonight. I shall meet you half an hour before midnight over there, and he pointed toward the hills where the evergreen woods spread. "Where the woods begin you will find a small trail leading into the underbrush. Stand behind trees till I come."

Jubilantly I pressed his hand and thanked him profoundly. Then I asked him to take the ferry back, for we had no reason to cross to the other side. Our mission had been accomplished.

Time dragged by as we wandered aimlessly around. We must not draw attention to ourselves. The less a person was noticed by the soldiers, the better. As soon as it was dark enough we made our way to the woods. We knew we would have to wait, but we wanted to find the assigned meeting place. Undisturbed, we crossed fields and meadows and after some searching found the brush trail. We stepped under the trees and waited. After a while we noticed that we were not alone. Many silent figures stood under the dripping trees as we did and waited. I whispered, "How will the man take such a large group across without being detected?" Micherle shrugged her shoulders.

We had another worry on our minds. Would the guide really come? What if he didn't? We had given him all we owned. What if he betrayed us after collecting our stuff?

More people arrived, among them women with children, even babies. The night was dark and foggy and it drizzled. How did those mothers keep their little ones from protesting loudly about the unearthly hour and the cold rain? Maybe the guide has advised the mothers what to do, for all the babies had diapers tied around their mouths, with their noses left open for breathing. This muffled their little voices sufficiently for safety. Preschool children held tightly to their mothers' hands or skirts, not daring to whisper or cough.

What a relief when the guide finally appeared! He whispered orders, and the group lined up in single file. Information from the front would be given by signs, which were to be passed on from one person to the next. He briefly explained the route and some landmarks that marked the border over which we would have to run. Then the silent figures began to move forward, led by that rough-looking man who was willing to risk his hide either for the pay he received or because he felt called to help. I didn't know why, and it didn't matter as long as he was doing it.

61

Our progress was slow because every step had to be cautious and noiseless. Flashlights could not be used (most of us did not own such a luxury anyway), and the guide led us part of the way through dense underbrush where it was hard, especially for the mothers with children, to move without noise. Micherle and I were near the rear, while the mothers with children were in the middle of the line so we could give a hand once in a while. We had already walked for a long, long time and I wondered if these woods would ever come to an end. I began to worry also because I could see the first signs of dawn. Several times I had run into trees in the foggy darkness. Micherle limped; she had twisted her ankle when she stepped into a hole. But she kept going, for small pains count for little in such times of danger and suspense.

Then came the sign which indicated that the Russian patrol line was only meters away. Now we were again on our own because here the ferryman had to leave us to make his way back. Now each of us would try to break through the brush to cross the border line. Micherle stood close to me waiting for my signal to run.

Suddenly we heard Russian guards shouting, "*Stoj! Stoj! Stoj* [Stop]!" Next we heard shots followed by screams and then soldiers' cursing and shouting. I threw myself flat on the muddy ground behind a bush, and Micherle lay close beside me, breathing heavily. The woods had opened its merciful arms and swallowed us up; we saw none of the others of our group. The shooting stopped, and all was silent again. Only our hearts beat so loudly that we felt the ground would transmit the sound to the enemy soldiers.

My thoughts raced: "Marianne, dumb girl, you ran into a trap. The Russians are in front of us. Shall we turn back?" Impossible! Morning was breaking, and we could never make it back through no-man's-land without being caught. This must be the end.

Suddenly we heard a child screaming. It was not far from us, calling for its mother. Dear me, why didn't those mothers watch their children better in an hour like this? This child would attract the soldiers. I worked my way toward the child, remaining flat on the ground while moving forward on my elbows and slightly bent knees.

The child was a skinny, frightened little girl, three or four years old, with blond wet strands of hair hanging over her shoulders. I closed her mouth tightly with my hand and whispered, "Be quiet, child! The Russians will find us if you scream so loud. Where is your mother?"

I took my hand from her mouth so she could talk. She sobbed softly as she told me that her mother had held her baby brother in one arm while she, the "big sister," had held Mother's other hand. When the shooting began, *Mammi* was suddenly gone and "big sister" found herself alone in the big dark woods.

"If you stop crying, honey, we shall see if we can't find *Mammi* somewhere. Come with me over to where my girl friend is waiting." I stroked her head and wiped her tears away, and we crawled cautiously back to Micherle.

Time was running out. Morning was moving in fast, and time would work against us if we didn't hurry. I looked at the strange child who had cuddled up with childlike confidence, trusting me to find her mother. We would have to run somewhere, but how could we run if we kept the child with us? On the other hand, could we leave her alone in the woods and run away?

"Listen, we will try to make it across the border," I decided. "We cannot go back, and we will be caught for sure here in no-man's-land. We must try for the American Zone."

I turned to the child. "*Häschen* [little rabbit], we will take you along. Maybe your mother made it across, and we will find her over there. Now, you must promise two things: you must run as fast as your little feet will carry you, and you must not make any noise. Do you think you can do that for me?"

The girl nodded gravely, without a word. She had already begun to keep her promise.

I showed Micherle how to get a fast grip on the child's hand

63

without hurting her wrist in case we had to pull her, then I took the child's other hand securely, and we began to run.

First we ran down the last meters to the foot of the wooded hill. Then we had to cross a small road running through the valley, which was the actual patrol line of the Eastern guards. After crossing a deep ditch by the road we entered an open grassy area without trees or bushes to protect us. We ran in desperation, expecting bullets to hit us any moment. At the meadow's end we came to a small creek whose waters looked swift and murky from the rains. We had no chance to guess the depth of the creek. We waded into the swift water and splashed across as fast as we could. Stumbling and struggling, our main concern was to keep the child's head above the water and keep our balance. As we struggled ashore at the other side, ice-cold water ran in little streams down our hips and legs, and our coats clung heavily to us. We reached some woods again and started running uphill. We knew that the American patrol line was at the top of the hill.

Partway up, I threw myself down in exhaustion. "I have to rest awhile," I gasped. "I can't go on another step even if the Russians are after us!" Micherle had lain down too, breathing in short, sharp intervals.

Why hadn't the Russians shot at us? I wondered. We had been perfect targets. Why did we get through unmolested? I could think of no answer. Did the soldiers see us and take pity on the little child between us? Soldiers may be cruel when drunk, but perhaps they have tender hearts when sober. Most of them love children. I had seen Russians share their lunch with hollow-cheeked begging children more than once. Maybe the officer in charge was a father himself and hadn't been able to shoot when he saw those little legs running in despair!

My eyes fell upon the child. For a moment I had forgotten her! There she stood, dripping wet from neck to water-filled shoes. Her little body shook, and her teeth chattered. Tears rolled down her cheeks, drawing straight lines on the mud-smeared face. But no loud sob escaped her blue lips; she wept noiselessly and waited without complaint. Why must little tots suffer so much? I wondered.

"Quick, Micherle, pull something out of my knapsack. There should be something dry on top. We must change the child's coat or she will catch pneumonia for sure." Hastily I pulled off the child's dripping coat and wrapped her in my dry sweater.

Overtired, she snuggled herself trustingly on my shoulders. What else could I do but pick her up and carry her? Micherle put my knapsack over one of my shoulders and then we began to climb the hill again. The child fell asleep, and with the extra load I had to use all my willpower to keep going. One step, one more, one again—will the top of the hill never come? What if the soldiers should catch us just a few meters short of the goal? "Don't think, Marianne, just keep going!"

Suddenly we had arrived! We had actually crossed over without a scratch. Carefully I laid the child down for a moment and turned to look eastward. The dark evergreens stretched away for miles, and somewhere in those dark woods were my pursuers. Death and I had met again, and I had been spared. Why?

I bent over and looked into the child's white face. Her closed eyelids flickered, and shivers shook the undernourished little form. Gently I lifted her from the damp ground and turned to the west. I knew I had to find help fast if that child were to survive, and I was determined to find it. In the distance blinked a light.

"Let's go toward the light," I urged. "Maybe somebody will take the child in."

Steadying ourselves, we lifted the child and began to walk again, across fields and pastures, over rocks and little streams. The light came nearer while the dawn yielded to a new day.

Yes, there was to be a dawn even after the darkest, longest night; for light is stronger than darkness, and life is stronger than death.

5—I.C.G.

New Horizons

If I hadn't been so tired I would have noticed it. But I didn't; neither did Micherle! As we approached the building with the light, it did not register on our minds that the building was not a German farmhouse. I only knew I couldn't carry that child another step, and that the child was deathly pale.

I stepped up to the door and knocked. No reply. I started to beat the door with my fist, determined not to let up until somebody answered. Maybe if the farmer family could see the child, they might be willing to help. All I wanted was a warm place where the child might get dry.

Unexpectedly the door opened, and there stood an American soldier. I knew he was an American. I had seen pictures of such soldiers during the war while I trained as a Nazi. I didn't remember much that I had been taught about those men, only two things; American men, living in big dirty cities, were all shooting gangsters, and they chewed gum!

The soldier before me stood tall, armed—and chewing! "What do you want?" he drawled, rolling his gum between his teeth.

I was petrified with fear, and my scared face must have spoken louder than my German words as I stuttered and mumbled my plea. I knew no English at all, and obviously the soldier did not understand my German. He gave me a puzzled look, then turned and called a name. Presently an interpreter appeared and asked me in German what we wanted.

"We just crossed over from the Russian side, and we found this child alone in the woods," I explained. "We had to cross the river and the child got soaked up to her head. She will die unless

67

The little girl did not sob. Why must tots suffer? I wondered.

we can get her warm and dry. And please tell that soldier that he should not send us back to the Russians—" The child had buried her face on my shoulder and sobbed silently.

The next thing that happened I had never thought possible, not even in my dreams and imaginations. The door opened wide and we were invited in! Other soldiers appeared and brought a cot and blankets. They told me to wrap a blanket around the child and remove her wet clothing. Then we laid the cold little form on the cot. Meanwhile, another soldier had brought a big cup of hot chocolate. As I lifted the child's head up, she sipped the drink eagerly and greedily. Slowly I watched the color come back into her face, and her cold hands loosened their tight grip on my fingers. Gently I put her head back and told her to go to sleep. She nodded, and I stepped back into the corner where Micherle stood.

But some of the soldiers began to talk to the child. It was a strange language, to be sure, but it sounded as if they were trying to talk baby talk. They made funny faces and rolled their eyes like clowns. She sat up and watched. After a while she had lost her shyness and talked happily with those strange big boys. They had a big time together in spite of the fact that they could not understand each other's words.

I stood in my corner and watched, mystified. How could this all be true? Through ignorance, we had run into a situation where we were at the mercy of American soldiers, our enemies. They had taken us in and helped the child; now they were entertaining her, laughing and jumping. Why would gangsters, who hated the Germans so badly that they had come across the ocean to fight us, treat us so kindly? This had to be a big trap, but it didn't look like a trap. It seemed so real! Did I dare to think that Americans were not gangsters, just friendly human beings? Maybe I had been misinformed. Again I had the feeling that something was breaking within me. Yes, my previous concept of American people was crumbling. Goebbels's hateful propaganda was proving to be lies again.

At last the little girl fell asleep, and the soldiers became quiet. Some had tiptoed away, and the others stood beside the cot. I stepped forward and looked down at the resting child. Well, we had accomplished what we had tried to do, and it was time for Micherle and me to leave again. The child seemed to be in good hands. I nodded a shy *Danke* and made for the door.

Before I reached it, a soldier spoke up. He motioned and tried to make me understand something. He rubbed his eyes and asked, "Are you tired, sleepy—you want to sleep too?"

So that was it! Soldiers were all alike, I thought. I shook my head in disgust and backed toward the door. "*Nein, nein, Danke,*" I whispered hoarsely.

The soldier seemed to read my thoughts. "Look," he said proudly, and pointed toward himself, "I American." His big chest seemed to widen several centimeters! He spoke slowly and deliberately, and I nodded. I understood. Yes, he was an American!

"I no Russian." He pointed toward the east and shook his head emphatically.

I nodded again. No, he was not a Russian!

"I good man." He grinned and showed his big white teeth.

I started in surprise! Was he really good? Each of us knew what the other was thinking.

He went to a door, opened it, and motioned us to enter. We saw two cots with blankets in a small room. Most likely it was one of their first-aid rooms. He nodded, gesticulated, and rubbed his eyes again. "You sleepy, go rest. We—good men."

I hesitated again. It was against common sense to trust, and I knew it was better to turn and run. But somehow I couldn't! Those cots looked so-o-o-o good, the blankets so dry and warm, my eyes so heavy. I had been running away from everything for many weeks. I was so tired of running. Yes, I would take a chance and lie down and sleep while all those soldiers swarmed around. It was foolish to trust, but I would do it anyway.

With a trace of a smile I looked into the eyes of our host and nodded slowly. Politely he held the door open and ushered us in, then he closed the door carefully and was gone. Without further delay we threw ourselves onto those cots and spread the blankets over us. We went to sleep within minutes.

I do not know how long we had slept when a loud knock on the door made me jump. Frightened, I called, "Who is it? What do you want?"

In stepped a soldier in white, who proved to be an American army cook. His face was round, full, and pink. He looked healthy and pleasant. He smiled broadly, and that made his face rounder and fuller yet. A high white cap towered over his head. At the middle he seemed to be round and full also; a white apron covered a lot of waist. In his arms he carried a tray loaded with food. He put the tray down and asked with a jolly wink, "You want to eat?"

Hardly believing my ears and eyes, I nodded. We were supposed to eat something! I looked at the tray. It was loaded with food. I wondered which of all these things we would be permitted to eat. Obviously the man would eat with us. I looked into his face and waited for him to give further orders.

"Eat," he urged again, as we hesitated.

"*Alles* [all of it]?" I asked breathlessly.

"Yeah, all." He seemed amused.

"*Danke! Danke!*"

He grinned and left the room.

Our hands shook as we reached for the food. I tried to butter my bread. I had never seen snow-white bread before; the rye bread of my country had been dark and coarse. White baked goods were called *Kuchen* (cake). Why, I wondered, would American soldiers begin their day eating cake with butter and jelly, besides all the other things, some of them strange to us, just for a simple meal like breakfast! Puzzling or not, this food was tastier and fancier than anything we had eaten for many weeks, and there was so much! We also had pots of steaming coffee. It was a new taste. I had only known grain coffee before, and the new taste was tangy and bitter. But it was a drink, anyway; and it warmed us inside. When we picked up the last few crumbs, we wiped our mouths with paper napkins. What a luxury! Napkins! Unheard of in postwar Germany. Maybe we were only imagining things!

We stretched out on the cots and tried to sleep again. The cook had come in to take the empty tray away and had motioned that we should go back to sleep. But sleep would not come, and I felt disgusted with myself. To have a chance to sleep for a few hours under real covers, in a real house, and then to lie awake! I didn't know much about coffee then.

"Let's get up," I finally suggested, so we did. We folded the blankets neatly and fished through our knapsacks for some dry clothing. Our skirts were still damp and terribly wrinkled, so we changed into our *Dirndls*, typical German garments of pleated wide skirts with white blouses and special bodices. We put white socks on and brushed our tangled hair long and carefully. We felt like new people! Stepping out into the hall, we looked around to find somebody we could say our *Danke* to once more before leaving.

The interpreter asked us to come into the office. The officer in charge greeted us with a polite nod of his gray head, and spoke rapidly. Then the interpreter said in German, "The lieutenant has contacted the Russian headquarters across the border to get some information about the child you brought in. The Russians knew about the lost child, for they caught the mother with the baby. We offered to return the child to the Russian border so it could be given back to its mother, but the Russians refused to take her back in order to punish the mother.

"We cannot keep the little girl with us here in the barracks," the interpreter continued apologetically. "It's not the right place for her. Our office has contacted the International Red Cross in the next village. They have promised to take care of the child. Will you kindly take her to the next village and deliver her to the Red Cross lady there?"

The little girl was brought in. Somebody had been kind enough to wash and comb her hair, and her clothing was dry. She smiled radiantly and showed us her new possessions. Her pockets were filled with candies and crackers. After another thank-you, we took the child's hand and started to leave. As we walked toward the entrance, somebody called once more. The interpreter told us, "The lieutenant said you should go right away to the office window at the Red Cross station; don't stand in line!"

"Yes, thank you," I answered. I didn't know what he meant.

I understood an hour later, after we arrived in the village and found the Red Cross refugee office. People stood in line for blocks! I remembered the parting words of the German interpreter and marched boldly by the long rows of refugees, who watched us with critical eyes.

Before anybody could stop me, I said, "Please, madam, an American officer said I should come right away up to your window and bring you this little girl because—"

"Come right in," said the uniformed lady, opening the door. In we marched, while hundreds looked on and perhaps silently protested.

"Sit down," encouraged the nurse, and settled herself behind the desk.

What was happening all around us? Refugees were not treated like this. Nobody had bothered to offer us a chair or food or shelter for so long. Suddenly everybody seemed to be nice. First, the Americans giving us food and sleep, now the lady with the Swiss accent treating us like people. All these foreign people seemed to be so human and kind.

"You girls," she smiled, "the American lieutenant told me over the telephone about you and the child. I want you to know that we respect you highly for saving the child while you were running for your lives. It was wonderful of you to take her with you."

"*Schwester*" (nurses in Germany are called "sister"), I answered, embarrassed, "we didn't do anything special. I mean, we couldn't have left the little thing all alone in the dark woods, could we?"

"No, dear, you couldn't have left her in the woods, but many *would* have left her. We are glad that you didn't."

I smiled down at my little friend. As usual, she held tightly onto my hand or skirt and seemed to be content as long as she could stay near me. I stroked her hair while she cuddled close.

The lady continued. "We have a little problem, girls. The International Red Cross office in W. (the next large city) is trying to make arrangements for the child, but every *Heim* [emergency shelters for refugee children] is overfilled; no bed is available. It will take a few days to make room somewhere for your little foundling, and I am wondering if you two girls would be willing to take care of her until we find a place."

"But, *Schwester*," I interrupted, "we are more than willing to do so, only we have absolutely nothing for her! We gave all our valuable things to the guide who led us across no-man's-land. We have no food, no shelter, no clothing for the child, nothing. I can keep her by my side, but I can't give any care."

"Oh, I forgot to mention," the nurse interrupted kindly, "that the Red Cross will provide what is needed. We will register you."

She reached for her fountain pen and some forms. "We will give all three of you ration cards for a week and some money, and I will call the hotel and tell them to give you shelter until we call you again."

Had I heard right? That woman offered us a hotel room, food, and money just because we would baby-sit a little refugee? After filling out some information blanks, she reached for the telephone and reserved a room in the only hotel of the village, which had been taken over by the occupation army. We received ration cards and money and left the office.

When we stepped out, some refugees who stood in line surrounded us and asked some eager questions. "How come you girls got to go in without waiting?" asked a haggard, tired-looking woman, while trying to keep her children in check, who fussed and kicked around her. I told the story briefly.

"How lucky can somebody be?" said one man. "Do you realize

73

that it usually takes people eight to ten days to register, be approved, and get a ration card? And here you girls crossed the border just last night and are all taken care of already." We smiled apologetic smiles and left hurriedly. We had no longing to get tangled up with long lines of people who had waited for days and couldn't help resenting our streak of luck.

We walked to the hotel and found our room with beds ready. I put the little girl down for a nap and sat beside her until she went to sleep. So we had tried to help a lost child! Suddenly that child had become our talisman. How strange! We had not saved her because we expected any reward, but it seemed almost as if life was rewarding us for the deed. Kindness, I thought, must beget kindness, and hate will beget hate. Every thought, every action brings forth after its own kind.

For three days and nights we enjoyed the comfort of the hotel room. We used our ration cards and the money sparingly, but we slept plentifully and felt refreshed and rested. On the third day the Red Cross sent a message. A place had been secured, and we had to bring the child back to the Red Cross office. I did so with mixed feelings. We had become attached to each other, and the child didn't want to leave me. Furthermore, I did not want to give her up. But we had to be glad that she would be taken care of, and I tried to comfort her. Tears flowed freely as we hurried away. The last sound we heard was of the nurse trying to still the girl's screaming.

I never again heard of the child. Besides, I have forgotten her name, but I have thought of her often and wondered what might have become of her. Did she ever rejoin her mother? Did her soldier daddy ever come back from the war? Only eternity will give me the answers, so I must wait.

We strapped up our knapsacks, handed the key of the hotel room to the doorkeeper, and walked out. We were on our own again. Following the country road to the southwest, we wandered along without plans. After all, we had it made; we had arrived in the West. We had our refugee registration cards which assured us we could request another ration card every ten days, and even though this meant only a minimum of food, this would protect us from starvation.

What to do next? For weeks we had been urged on by one goal only—the West. Now that we had made it, we felt like boats without rudders. We began to drift. We walked slowly, passed many other refugees on every road, entered villages, and learned little tricks to make the ration cards last longer.

We saw unmistakable signs of new beginnings. In different places the people in the villages had already begun to rebuild. Children, women, and old men were busy among ruins, carrying rubbish away, scraping old bricks for reuse, mixing clay and straw for new bricks. Some stores had reopened to supply the few needs which could be supplied. Some restaurants were beginning to serve food to the milling refugees if they had ration cards and money. Every so often we treated ourselves extravagantly and bought a bowl of hot soup, though this took a big section out of our ration cards. Some drugstores had reopened, too, and tried to do business with almost nothing. They offered herbs and a limited supply of medicine to distribute for real emergencies. These supplies came from the occupation army. They also had worthless knickknacks on display for the eager refugees. It was almost an obsession with some of the homeless wanderers like us; they had to buy everything which was "free"—in other words, without ration cards. It had become a habit for people to stroll through every drugstore looking eagerly for "free" merchandise. Once we were lucky enough to find a store where they sold cough drops without prescription. The stuff tasted horrible, but what did it matter? They filled the stomach for a while.

We arrived at a certain village, fair-sized, and not damaged by the war. As we wandered along the main street, we discovered a pharmacy. The urge was irresistible, as usual, to go in and try our luck. We kept our money supply up by selling part of our ration cards to people with more means, so we always had enough money. As we entered the dim old place, we noticed another young woman standing at the counter, talking to the white-haired pharmacist. Obviously they knew each other. Those villagers, we thought, had the advantage. They knew the people behind the counters and were favored over strangers. Well, that was life!

Micherle and I looked around and searched. Any offers which would be of any use to us? Nothing we could see. Well, we could ask for cough drops. We approached the man and asked politely for them.

At the sound of my voice the young woman looked up in surprise and stared at me. I stared back into two surprised brown eyes. I had seen that person before!

"Annemarie! What in the world are you doing here?"

Annemarie was Rudy's sister, and we had been the best of friends while I had visited in Rudy's home. We had not heard from each other since I had returned my ring to their mother, and I had often wondered what had become of her. I only knew that the Russians and Polish had taken over her homeland, Silesia.

Annemarie stretched her hands out, and I took them in mine. She was not able to talk at once, as tears brimmed in her eyes. We walked out of the building, Annemarie leading the way. Little by little we began to piece our stories together. Annemarie cried while she talked, and every bit of my resentment fled as I listened. She and her parents had lost everything; they had saved nothing but their lives. Father Hirschmann had caught pneumonia and had been near death for weeks. Mother had nursed him day and night. Food had been scarce, and the valuable things they had carried had to be traded for milk and medicine.

"Marianne," Annemarie sobbed, "you wouldn't recognize Mother anymore! She lost sixty pounds in six weeks. Father still looks like a shadow; he is so thin and pale, and he cannot climb stairs. We live out in the country because a kind woman opened her house to us and gave us an upstairs room. We are luckier than many because we have a roof over our heads and a bed for Father!"

For a moment I had to fight it-serves-you-right feelings. Then

I felt ashamed of even thinking such thoughts. There was no need to feel good because Rudy's rich family had suddenly become poor, and we were all in the same boat. Deepest pity filled me as I looked at Annemarie. She had been the sheltered, overprotected girl of a well-to-do home, and not even the war had inconvenienced her too severely during the first four years. I tried to picture her fright and agony when they had fled from home. She looked so skinny and forlorn as she walked beside me pushing her landlady's bicycle.

"Annemarie," I said, "please take my heartiest greetings to your parents. Tell them that I have nothing against them anymore and that I wish you all best of luck." Swallowing my pride with great effort, I added, "And, Annemarie, may I ask you how your brother is?"

"Oh, Marianne, don't you know?" Her eyes overflowed again. "Rudy is—dead for all we know." She proceeded to tell me why they thought so—lost boat, no mail for months—

Rudy dead? Yes, I had hoped he would be, because it was so hard to think he might be suffering in a prisoner-of-war camp. But now that I heard his sister say so, I knew that I had lied to my heart. No, I didn't want him to be dead! Life had become almost hopeful again since I had crossed over to West Germany, and I had to admit to myself that I had looked for him constantly ever since I had escaped my persecutors. I had studied lists of registered names in every Red Cross station. I had looked in every man's face in the hope of finding Rudy among the refugees. I had really begun to hope again because my heart refused to give up. My buried love had pushed and inspired me to wander on, to search, to find—to find *him*.

I had to be alone for a few moments because I was too proud to show how much I cared. Stopping, I tried to smile at Annemarie while I said: "Annemie [her nickname], I think Micherle and I should go back to town and let you bicycle home, or your mom might be worried. It was so good to see you again, and please do not forget to tell your mother I have no bitterness in

77

my heart toward her. It is the least we all can do for Rudy, to make peace and forget the past."

Annemarie and I shook hands, and we parted. Micherle walked silently with me back to the village.

Rudy was dead, most likely. Well, again that cruel, miserable little bit of hope, that could keep people in agony for years, preyed on my mind. What did it really matter? He wasn't mine anymore even if he still lived. A wave of despair and hopelessness swept over me. Was it worthwhile to keep going even here in the West? It was almost more than my pride could bear to realize that my main purpose in going on had been my hidden hope to find Rudy.

A familiar voice called me. I turned around. In the distance I saw a girlish figure on a bicycle pushing the pedals as hard as she could while waving her hand and calling. It was Annemarie coming after us at top speed. Breathless, she pulled up to where we stood. "Marie Anne," she pleaded, "my mother would like to see you. As soon as I told her, she sent me right back after you. Please, Marianne, come and visit with my parents."

Now I felt resentful. It was one thing to send a kind message— But it was another to go and see her, shake her hand, talk to her. What if I said the wrong thing? How far could I go in forgiving her before my hurt pride would take over? What if I tried to get even with her for her heartlessness in breaking us up?

My face must have shown my struggle, for Annemarie said softly, while her eyes pleaded, "Please, Marianne, come with me. Mother has changed, and if she wronged you, she has paid for it in more ways than one. You don't know how much it would mean to her to see you. Please, for Rudy's sake, come!"

I felt ashamed of myself. Surely I would go and see those two poor old sick people if they wanted me to. Why should I add to their sorrow by refusing? We turned again and walked with Rudy's sister until we reached a small village surrounded by hills and woods. Steeling myself, I climbed some stairs to their place.

Seconds later I stood before two people whom I hardly recognized. Though hardly able to hide my shock at their appearance, I ran toward the mother and put my arms around her. She could not speak for a while, as she and Dad began to cry. She seemed to know what I was thinking and tried to smile. "Yes, my girl, I know we have changed. Life has dealt hard with all of us. Come and sit down!"

She had food ready for us, bless her heart, and the old Silesian hospitality! She had gone to the landlady and asked for two eggs. That took a lot of courage. Some bread was ready also.

I could hardly eat, for I knew that they needed the food for themselves. The father was blue-lipped and short of breath and cried every time he began to talk. My last feeling of resentment melted in pity. Rudy's name was scarcely mentioned. Neither side felt free to talk about him.

As we got up to leave, Mother squeezed my hand. "Marie-anne," she said sadly, "I didn't mean to hurt you, and I did not know that my boy loved you so deeply. He tried to find you again, but you never answered!"

"Let's forget the past," I said quietly, "and be friends again. Even if Rudy were still alive, he and I would never be able to get together again for marriage, but I would like to be friends with you for the rest of my life."

"Please, my girl, write as soon as mail will go again and you have a regular address, for you might be all Rudy left us, if he is dead." Father's blue lips quivered.

I nodded. "I will write to you," I promised, and kissed all three good-bye. Micherle and I climbed down the stairs and stepped out into the evening. Micherle, shy around strangers, hadn't said much, but as soon as we were alone, she started to chatter. The food had excited her most. To think that we each had eaten an egg, fried! We had forgotten how good eggs tasted. What nice people!

That night we found a barn in the fields and slipped in for the night. The next morning I knew that the time had come to make a decision. "Micherle," I said, "this lingering around is no good for us. I think we should leave this area and tramp to the South. I've longed to see the Alps all my life. Let's go and see southern Bavaria."

"Let's go!" said Micherle excitedly. After several days of walking, and after bumming part of the way on some freight trains, we neared Munich.

I was getting more and more disgusted with myself. All my life I had dreamed of a visit to the beautiful land in southern Germany. Now, while finally approaching it, I didn't feel anything at all. Something had gone very wrong with me lately, and I couldn't figure it out. It was as if all feeling had left me.

Did Micherle notice my changed behavior? I hardly bothered when she told me that she had met a young refugee and he had asked her to go along with him to Heidelberg. It didn't matter; nothing mattered anymore. I nodded, and she left! Well, now I was alone! No more responsibility, no more need to talk to anybody.

There seemed to be no hope or help for me, and I was beyond the point of recognizing my need for help and trying to find it somewhere. Most likely nobody would have cared anyway. No doctors or nurses were available for all those thousands of refugees in every city. People either survived or went *kaput*.

Years later I told a doctor about those days, and he told me I had been at the verge of a complete breakdown.

There was no way out, it seemed, and nobody cared. Nobody? Somebody must have cared and guided, for I can't believe that what took place one day was mere accident. I had forgotten God, but had He forgotten me?

A few days after my arrival in Munich I found myself, early in the morning, on a street. My beclouded mind was wrestling. Darkness seemed to press in from every side, and my head tried in vain to think. Past and present seemed to blend.

Was there still war? No, war had been over for five months. A strange silence covered the land. No more hammering of machine guns, no more explosions, no hostile droning of airplanes during the nights, no more screams and wild cries as bombs found their targets. It was so unbelievably still, so oppressively calm.

But the big city carried the unconcealed wounds and marks of recent destruction. Ruins and fire-blackened trees edged the avenues, throwing long, strange shadows in the new morning light.

I wandered aimlessly through the streets. The stricken city tried to awaken. Bricks and rubbish had been pushed to the sides, making a path for the crowds. People rushed and pushed eagerly to get to shops and counters where they would stand in line for hours to buy a few morsels of food, if luck stayed by. Working people made their way to their places of labor, streetcars overfilled with passengers clanged and banged impatiently. Bicyclists squeezed through throngs of pedestrians, frustrated and encumbered.

I stood and watched. There was no need for me to force my way; I had nowhere to go. With thousands of others I called "home" a little straw-covered square on the gym floor of an old half-destroyed school. And I was fortunate to have found even that.

Having received my morning food, a bowl of thin soup and two pieces of dry bread, I was free to go and do as I pleased. Nobody cared if I didn't check in by nightfall, and many more new "numbers" waited for a vacant place on the straw. And still more refugees flooded in from the East.

I watched the morning rush, studying passing faces—strange emotionless faces, seemingly hard and unfeeling, without a smile. The memory of death and the present hunger were stamped on their sad eyes and bony cheeks. But it mattered little to me. I didn't expect a smile, not even a spoken word.

Looking up, surprised, I felt the sudden warmth of the sun through my thin, shabby jacket. Why was the sun shining? It had rained for so many weeks. Almost at every step of my westward flight, rain had drenched me mercilessly. Now the bright,

81

cheery sun and those charred ruins around me didn't seem to fit together. I stood staring and wondering, trying to bring order into my muddled brain. My mind turned in senseless rotation the words *sun, rain, ruins, death, hunger.*

Oh, yes, I was hungry again! The two pieces of old bread did not last long enough, let alone the watery soup. Why, now, why did the sun shine?

A deep urge crept up my throat, an urge to cry, to let go, to feel again. But I could not do it; my smile and my tears seemed buried under an avalanche of horror. Oh, how much I wanted to feel those warm drops rolling down my cheeks. I tried and tried again, but I just couldn't cry. With a hopeless shrug of my shoulders I walked on.

Suddenly my eyes were caught by several printed announcements. Big letters notified the people that there would be a sacred concert that night. But where? At the far outskirts of the city stood a frail cathedral, cracked but still standing; the bombs must have missed it. Even the organ was still intact. A group of courageous string musicians were inviting everyone to the "Requiem" by Handel.

Music! Music? How long had it been since I had heard the sound of good music? It seemed so long ago, almost an eternity. Music belonged to a past world, a world I had no place or part in anymore.

Would the people let me in? The sign said everybody was welcome. And what about money? I had none to spare. I had given everything of value to the guide who had led me across to the border. I had saved nothing but my life and the knapsack on my back.

I read the invitation again: "Free Entrance—No Admission Fee!"

This was unbelievable. Why would anything be free? Why would anyone make music for *me*, voluntarily? I pondered the mystery. Yes, there would be a concert, real music, which I loved so much.

New Horizons

Suddenly I was part of the crowd. I pressed forward, elbowed my way into a streetcar, and asked with new self-confidence for the way to the cathedral. Surprisingly enough, people were willing to direct me without so much as a frown. I swallowed hard in astonishment.

For several hours I lingered around the cathedral until the people came and filed reverently, expectantly into the high, arched sanctuary. The air inside was heavy with incense.

Not daring to sit in a pew, I stood lonely and still with the latecomers. The building eventually was filled. My eyes searched wonderingly about the church. Everything seemed unfamiliar and different. I looked up and followed the curving lines of the Romanesque dome.

The entire inner ceiling was covered with an old painting. I recognized it as a reproduction of the famous Sistine Chapel ceiling, "The Creation of Adam" by Michelangelo. God is reaching out to Adam. As His finger touches the finger of Adam, the spark of life enters the newly created form of the man, and he becomes a living soul.

Yes, I knew the picture, but I had forgotten the implication. As I gazed up, my mind struggled to get hold of something I had learned long ago at Mother's knee—something that had been part of my childhood. What was it that I tried to remember? Was I looking for something?

Suddenly the music began. Strings and organ blended softly and harmoniously. The sound swelled, becoming louder and stronger, filling the old building, ascending to the dome, embracing the old cracked picture and finally bursting out through the broken, stained-glass windows with joyful ringing into the wide star-filled night.

Suddenly I remembered the story of the picture. Mother told it again, and I listened. Standing alone among the hundreds of quiet strangers, I suddenly felt warm within me. The ice in my innermost being broke. The music and Mother's words forced their way through the cracks of my broken soul. My eyes grew suddenly moist, and my heart began to sing. Hot tears of joy rushed down my face, but not wanting to disturb the other listeners, I did not lift my hand to wipe my face. My heart cried out, "Mother, I can feel again; oh, Mother, where are you?"

When the music came to its glorious finale, I gazed up again. In the painting, God looked lovingly and longingly at Adam, and the man looked adoringly into God's eyes. But somehow they both seemed to look down at me, and I imagined I saw their eyes smiling.

Slowly I moved out, as the surging crowd caught me and carried me through the large doorway in the back. Then I found myself under the dark, velvety night sky and looked up again.

My mind was still searching and asking questions. There were so many things I could not understand, but it did not matter anymore. My heart had tasted again one moment of peace. Maybe life had had a purpose after all, and maybe there was lasting peace somewhere, a peace I had known before and lost. Maybe I could go out and find it again. At least I could try!

I nodded a grateful good-bye to the dome of the cathedral, where the lights were going out one by one over the picture of God and Adam. I turned around, straightened up, and with new courage walked into the night through the ruins and rubbish. My heart sang, and it was a new song. Or was it an old, long-forgotten song?

Beginnings?

CHAPTER 7

The world looked different when I woke up the next morning. The inner pressure had eased, and when I closed my eyes I could again see the picture and hear the beautiful music. As I wandered through the city, I found things I had not seen before. Autumn had come and, stepping over the majestic Alps, had begun to paint the land in bright and happy colors, even in the damaged city. The sun seemed to apologize for all the rain of the summer, for the Indian summer brought bright sunshine, deep blue skies, and fleecy white clouds. I had found a small park with benches, trees, and bushes left, and from there I watched the clouds, breathed in the pure air, and listened to the busy noises of a resurrecting city.

Other refugees had discovered those benches too, and as we met over and over again, we began to nod shy greetings. Refugees are usually not the most sociable people, so I looked up surprised when one day a young man walked up beside me and introduced himself politely. Decent girls, I believed, did not make acquaintances with men in the streets. *Strassenbekanntschaften* (street acquaintances) were for cheap girls only. I raised my eyebrows in surprise and wondered what to do. Maybe it was the music still ringing in my heart, maybe the smiling blue sky or the white clouds that tumbled dreamily with the wind; but this time I smiled and answered with a few friendly words. He was a refugee also, from my homeland besides, and after a short time we had become friends. How nice!

Suddenly Gerhard, my new acquaintance, asked, "Miss Appelt, did you say you had educational training during the last years?"

85

"Yes," I nodded, "one could put it that way if necessary."

He got enthusiastic. "Do you know that you might be able to find a job? The State Department of Education and Culture here in Munich is looking desperately for elementary-school teachers. Maybe you could apply."

I shook my head. "No, sir, I have no chance. They will not hire Nazi leaders; and I had a high rank in the Hitler Youth. They would catch up with me sooner or later; besides, I would not want to lie!"

"But you don't understand, *Fräulein*. They give amnesty to Hitler Youth members. As long as you were not a party member you will be OK."

Suddenly I was interested. No, I had not been a party member, only a member of the Hitler Youth movement. Somehow life had been so busy that our school had never found the time to stage the important ceremony of enrolling us in the party.

"No, I was not a party member, just a leader in the Senior Youth movement. But I have no papers with me to prove my education or anything. How would anybody hire me for any job?"

"Never mind, *Fräulein*. Try it anyway and see. You don't need to tell them everything anyhow! The new Bavarian government is determined to reopen at least the elementary schools by the first of October, and there is a great lack of teachers. Nazi members cannot be rehired, by order of the military government. You have nothing to lose, young lady; try it!"

He was right—I had nothing to lose. But how would I go about it?

He seemed to read my thoughts. "I will be glad to help you find the right office," he volunteered. "How about tomorrow morning?"

I smiled at his eagerness. Why was he so interested in helping me? It must be the same incomprehensible power that had compelled the American soldiers to help us, the Red Cross lady from Switzerland to organize refugee stations, the string musicians to make music for us—free. I couldn't understand it, but I had begun to accept it as something real and true even though I had no name for it.

Hitler had taught me many things: pride, perseverance, logic, morals, efficiency. But I did not consciously know what love was, kind neighborly love that cares without being forced to do so. The experience with my persecutors after the war had erased the remnants of my faith in humanity, and I could only wonder when someone showed me kindness.

"Yes," I heard myself saying, "I will meet you here tomorrow morning at nine o'clock. And thank you so much for your kindness."

The young man shook my hand, and we parted, smiling.

I found a way to iron my best dress, stood in a long line to wait my turn for a shower, and got my hair done in a beauty parlor after endless hours of waiting.

Arriving at our meeting place the next morning, I found the tall young *Landsmann* (man of my homeland) already waiting. He looked surprised and eyed me from head to toe.

"Do I look all right for that interview?" I felt uneasy under his searching gaze.

"Oh, yes," he said, blushing a little. "I think you look very nice."

Then it was my turn to blush, and we began to walk toward the center of the city.

He asked if he could meet me the next day to see how I fared. Then he gave me more advice on what to say, and left. I walked up some broad steps into a building.

I felt scared and lonely. In my hand I clutched a paper, the only document I possessed—my Catholic birth certificate. All I was able to prove was that I had been born, baptized, and named after my poor dead mother.

Presently I found myself seated across a desk from an elderly gentleman, who asked, in a friendly Bavarian drawl, "What do you want, my girl?"

I had planned my speech and reviewed it in my mind as I

tried to sleep on the straw-covered gym floor—but suddenly I couldn't say it! No, here again was someone kind, friendly, and human. Why should I try to deceive him?

I simply told the truth. I described my training, my bitter disappointment when I learned that the Nazis had lied, my lack of papers to prove anything. But I assured him I had a great desire to learn all over and be of service if given a chance.

I lifted my tear-filled eyes up and—was it possible? The man wasn't by any chance wiping his eyes! Why should he?

"Little girl," he said, "would you be willing to take a special examination before we make any further plans?"

"Oh, yes, I will be glad to!" I nodded eagerly, drying my eyes.

The man did some telephoning, and I was sent to different rooms for testing. In the afternoon I returned to the first office and the friendly old man received me smilingly.

"You did very well on your examinations," he said pleasantly. "Now for the other parts. We can give you an emergency certificate, and you will be included in a further training program while you teach, to prepare you for your final state examination. There is just one question left: What religion do you claim?"

I hesitated, not knowing what to say. Did I have any religion?

The man continued: "You see, Southern Bavaria is Catholic all the way through and the people resent teachers of other convictions."

"But, sir, I am a Catholic," I interrupted, and fumbled for my birth certificate.

"Can you prove it?"

I handed him my birth certificate. He studied it carefully, compared my application blanks and the document, stood up, and offered me his hand. "You are hired!"

I received further orders, a train ticket, and a letter of recommendation. I was to leave the next day.

I must have been dreaming again! No longer an unwanted refugee, I was a normal, respectable person again. Suddenly I was a teacher, hired by the democratic Bavarian government to teach the primary grades in Grossdingharding in the southern part of Bavaria. How could so many good things happen at once?

I met Gerhard the next morning to thank him and to tell him good-bye. He seemed sober and had a lonely look in his gray eyes, a look we refugees had learned to recognize as a part of our lives. I beamed and bubbled as I told him of my good fortune. We shook hands and parted. He looked sad. Weeks later it dawned on me that my leaving might have destroyed a small flame of hope in his own heart. He seemed to be such a pleasant person! Thank you, unknown friend, and good luck to you wherever you are! Our paths never crossed again.

The Alps towered in their beauty at the far southern end of the high plateau, which my train slowly crossed. My new school could not be reached directly by train; I had to walk several miles from the station. My principal received me in a very friendly manner after he had read the letter of introduction I handed him. He invited me to stay at his house until I found permanent lodging.

One unforgettable incident took place while I was a guest there. The principal's wife had served a simple supper, and I was invited. After the meal she took a large yellow apple from the cupboard and handed it to me. Overwhelmed by this gesture, I broke into tears. The lady looked perplexed.

"Ma'am," I stammered, "I think I have forgotten how an apple tastes. Would you permit me to save this apple for a few days so I could enjoy the smell?"

"You eat it," she said, "and I will give you another one when you leave!"

I could hardly get myself to eat that apple, that beautiful, lovely, aromatic piece of wonder. I had not seen, smelled, or eaten an apple since I left the hospital the year before, and I ate that apple with reverence. She forgot to give the second apple when I left her home—she had her cupboard full of apples—and my disappointment was so great that I had to fight back my tears.

Teaching was fun! It took a while to understand the Bavarian dialect of those little farmer children, but we enjoyed each other from the very first day. What a way of teaching it was, though! Even chalk had to be used with care, otherwise I would run out before the next ration came in. But we made satisfactory progress, and the parents seemed pleased.

There was one first-grade boy who, above the others, seemed to love me with all his little farmer heart. His parents had a little homestead near the school. He was the baby, born after the other children had grown up and left. Whenever I stepped out of the school building where I had my own little room upstairs, I would find him sitting on the front step waiting for me. I had made it a custom to go for a long walk every afternoon. After the rainy summer, the fall was unusually sunny and clear, and into November and December the days remained bright and pleasant. I never seemed to get enough of the beautiful view of the Alps, which I could see from my classroom window. My daily walks became my homage to that breathtaking scenery. My little friend, Sepperl, walked with me, his little hand slipped quietly in mine. He would talk or be silent, as he chose. His little heart worshiped his first-grade teacher, and my heart was warmed by his innocent affection.

One day, as I checked the homework, Sepperl had not done his assignment. "Sepperl," I said firmly, "if you don't do your homework you cannot go with teacher for walks anymore!"

His big blue eyes stared at me with a hurt expression. Slowly big tears covered the deep blue stars and rolled down the soft round cheeks. I quickly turned away.

"You've got to be firm, Marianne," I told myself, "or Sepperl will think he can get away with things because he is your little companion."

But those big, tear-filled blue eyes haunted me. After school I hurried to go for my walk so I could soften the blow for Sepperl. But Sepperl was not sitting on the steps as he usually did. "Well, maybe he is making up his homework," I mumbled, and went alone. The next morning Sepperl was not at school. Perhaps, like

Teaching was fun, though it took me a while to learn the Bavarian dialect.

some of the others, he had come down with the flu. Poor little fellow! I cut some pictures out for him during recess. I would go and take them to him in the evening.

When I came back from my walk, a messenger was waiting. Would I go right away to see Sepperl, please? He was critically ill.

My feet flew up the stairs to my room for the pictures, and then to Sepperl's house. As I entered the small, dark home, I heard the wailing of Sepperl's mother. My heart skipped a beat! Why was she wailing so loud? Didn't she know better? Sepperl needed quietness and rest! I stormed upstairs to his chamber and froze in horror. Candles had been lighted, and the mother and father knelt by his bed. Sepperl was dead.

Heartbroken, I threw myself over the little limp figure and cried, begged, pleaded, "Sepperl, wake up! Sepperl, it can't be true!"

But his face felt cold, and his eyes were closed. His little white hands were folded neatly and didn't move.

The parents led me downstairs and told me the story. They had thought he had a cold and had put him to bed. When the mother came back after a while to see how he was doing, he seemed to be choking. They sent for the doctor in the next town immediately. When after a few hours he arrived, he diagnosed it as diphtheria and could give little hope. The child suffocated. "He called for you, teacher," the mother sobbed, "but you were gone!"

I do not know how I managed to teach the next few days. At the funeral I sat with the relatives by request of the parents and sobbed so heartbrokenly that the mother tried to comfort me. Yes, she was a good Catholic, and she believed that the boy was in heaven. But I had no hope. True, I attended the Catholic mass because it was the thing to do in that community, but I couldn't believe most of their doctrines. I couldn't picture my Sepperl flying around as a little angel. All I could see was the withdrawn, grave, waxen face in a small white casket. And when I closed my eyes, I could see two big blue eyes as they had slowly filled with tears. Why? Oh, fate, why?

I lingered at his grave, not knowing what to do with myself. Suddenly I felt a strong hand taking mine and a friendly voice saying softly, "*Schulfräulein* [school miss], your grief will not bring him back. Don't cry anymore, please!"

Looking up, I saw two sincere blue eyes, a mass of curly blond hair, and white teeth in a big, boyish smile. It was one of the young farmers of the area to whom I had been introduced some weeks before at a wedding dance. We left the graveyard together and walked along the same path I had enjoyed so often with my little pupil. As the evening shadows lengthened, I began to tell him about that incident in class. Franzl listened patiently, then spoke. He was not a polished speaker, not a learned man. His hands were big, calloused farmer hands, used to holding the reins of a horse and following the plow. But his simple words comforted me more than any deep philosophy. My guilt and sorrow seemed to lift; and when I finally climbed the stairs to my room, I felt able to face life again.

He and I became fast friends. The community began to whisper as we appeared everywhere together. I was a little worried about the whole thing. One of his friends told me that Franzl's parents were giving him a hard time. He was the heir to one of the richest farms in the county, and I was as poor as a mouse in comparison.

At Christmas he brought me a piece of heirloom jewelry intended to be worn by the future wife of that family's heir. I was shocked! His mother had sent the gift to me. The son had won the family over, but was I ready?

Two weeks after Christmas I received an emergency visit from my supervisor. He urgently needed a new teacher for a village school twenty kilometers to the south. It was no easy job. Since the government had put a refugee camp into the former dance hall of that village, the number of students had grown too great for the school's single classroom, and I would have to

93

teach in two shifts. No books, no teaching help, eight grades, the responsibilities of a principal on top of the long teaching hours, dealing with the community and a stubborn school board—the job was enough to scare anyone. That's why my supervisor hadn't found a teacher for that place.

"Are you aware of my age, sir?" I asked.

"Yes, Miss Appelt." He bowed politely. "But I think you can do it!"

"I will try, if you will back me up," I promised.

The rest was not so easy. I packed my few belongings, visited a little snow-covered grave once more, and left a friendly community behind me—and a very unhappy young man.

Would my heart ever find a home again? I was not sure that I had been cut out to be a Bavarian farmer's wife. There was an old saying that Alpine flowers do not thrive well in other soil; and strange flowers, on the other hand, tend to wilt in the Alps. I knew I was a strange flower among the native girls, and they had let me know about it too!

Why had I accepted so hard a job? Maybe it had been a welcome escape. Maybe it was my nature. Certainly it was a challenge. I busied myself in my many new tasks from the day of my arrival. The *Bürgermeister* (mayor) of the village was understanding and friendly and helped me get started.

A few days later a fancy idea struck me. The neighboring village had not been able to reopen its school for lack of a teacher, and suddenly I thought of Annemarie, Rudy's sister, in northern Bavaria. We had exchanged letters after postal service had begun, and I knew she was looking for a job. I told my supervisor about her. He was enthusiastic, in spite of the fact that she was a Lutheran, and I invited her to come and visit me.

She was hired at once, and from the beginning we immensely enjoyed working together. We planned, tried new methods, helped each other in many problems, and roomed together in my school apartment. She was only one year older than I. The pupils made good progress, and the parents began to accept us as their friends. They customarily invited the two *Schulfräuleins* to weddings, dances, and church feasts. We were also known as good dancers, and our lives grew hectic with constant social events. Life had turned almost normal for us and even pleasant, except for shortages of material things, including food and clothing.

Into this calm water of everyday life a rock dropped—or was it a bomb? There had been a school holiday, and I had gone back to my former school community to visit friends. My blond farmer friend picked me up and insisted that I spend some time in his house. Knowing the custom of the land, I realized he was trying to compel me to make a decision. A boy didn't bring a girl home to his parents unless he had honest intentions of marriage. I felt uneasy, but yielded to his urging and visited with his parents.

While we made small talk, the telephone rang. Franzl answered and looked surprised. "It's for you, Marianne!"

"For me? Who would call me? Nobody knows I am at your house but Annemarie."

It was Annemarie. She had found a telephone in the mayor's office. She sounded choked and excited. "Marianne," she stuttered, "I just got a letter from my mother. The International Red Cross has found my brother. He is alive and on his way to see my parents. I know he will come down to see us. What shall I answer my mother?"

What should I say? Franzl stood beside me, waiting and wondering. My own heart and head seemed to spin like a wild carrousel. And Annemarie, at the other end of the line, was crying and laughing at the same time. I knew what it meant to her; she had worshiped her brother.

Well, I had to answer. "Tell your brother that he is more than welcome to visit you, Annemarie! After all, dear, he is the brother of my best girl friend, and I will accept him as such. Annemarie, I am so happy that he is alive. I know what it means to you and your family. You know my personal attitude; as long as he respects it, everything will be all right."

I Changed Gods

I had to be alone and collect my thoughts. I excused myself as soon as possible and in deepest turmoil returned home immediately. The past was coming alive again, and fear gripped me. But Annemarie bubbled over with joy. She had already sent a letter telling Rudy to come and had made a thousand plans.

He came! It was April, and a late snow had covered the land. Late in the evening, just as we were ready to retire, I answered a knock on the door and saw two men in navy-blue suits. Rudy stood before me, slim and haggard, while his friend, Riko, seemed to poke him from behind. Both looked cold and hungry.

"Welcome, and come in," I said with forced cheerfulness, and shook hands with both.

Our hearth beamed warmth, and we soon had hot food ready for the weary travelers. Rudy didn't say much, but sat quietly trying to warm his cold, wet feet. Annemarie was busy getting places ready for the boys to sleep, and I tried to keep conversation going. I couldn't help feeling sorry for Rudy. He had changed so much. All his young, self-confident assurance was gone, and he seemed depressed and lonely. I knew how he felt. His whole world had broken, just as mine had, only he had not yet managed to pick up the leftover pieces.

The tension eased after a few days, and Rudy and I slowly found a way to talk. I watched myself carefully so that my heart would not slip again, because I was more determined than ever not to fall in love with him again.

Rudy had just the opposite idea, as I found out later—too late. He was determined to win me back, and he did! It was a struggle, but his quiet determination (I call it stubbornness!) won. What else could I do? He needed me, and he loved me. The thought of marriage frightened me; I didn't feel ready for it. But we announced our engagement and found out that we had asked for trouble.

Rudy was a nominal Lutheran, I was a Catholic. Not a real Catholic; I didn't know what it was all about. Curiously, I had been baptized into that church as a result of a family squabble.

Beginnings?

My mother, a Seventh-day Adventist, had married my dad against the wishes of her parents. My dad, a harsh and bitter man, had no religion. After my birth he had compelled my mother to have me baptized into the Catholic Church. Furious because he was not able to shake her faith in her own beliefs, he insisted on my Catholic baptism just to prove his power. I had never been trained in the Catholic religion. When I had started as a teacher in southern Bavaria, I had quite a time adjusting myself. Carefully I had watched every movement of other churchgoers, learning the forms of Catholic worship and thus fitting myself into the community customs.

The priest of the area, a feared and respected figure, had never been too friendly. When I announced my engagement, he became our enemy. As was the custom, I had to attend a preparatory catechism for marriage. Since Rudy was not a Catholic, he did not attend these lectures, and I went alone.

"In twenty years of priesthood," the priest declared, "I have never married one of my Catholic sheep (he meant me, oh dear!) to a heretic."

I dreaded every lecture. He had another line against Rudy every time. The whole thing wore me down, since I was not sure I was doing the right thing anyway.

"Why do you want to marry Mr. Hirschmann anyhow?" he asked me one day. "You might lose your eternal reward and burn in hell!"

"Maybe I love him!" I replied rather heatedly.

"Why don't you marry one of the nice Catholic farmer boys from our area? You might not 'love' him, but you will finally have eternal life."

I resented this. This man knew how to touch my sorest spots too! The breaking up with my farmer friend had been one of my hardest moments since Sepperl's burial. Oh, for a mother or real friend to counsel with!

"Reverend," I said unhappily, "please try to understand. My fiancé needs me. I cannot let him go. He lost everything—his

97

home, his career, his future. He might go the wrong way if I turn my back on him. Can't you understand? There is a human responsibility."

But the man in the black robe couldn't understand. He only knew that Rudy was not one of his fold and that the wedding must be stopped. He threatened not to marry us. That would have been a catastrophe, because a ceremony before the judge only would not have been accepted as legal by the community. I had to get married in the Catholic church!

Rudy was not much help either. He still had some navy manners I did not fully appreciate. When I told him of my conversations with the priest, he became furious.

"Give that 'blackcoat' a message," Rudy steamed one day when he had come to visit me from Munich, where he studied at the university. "Tell that *Pfaff* that if he doesn't stop making trouble, I shall find him someday alone and beat him up good!"

"Do you really want me to tell this to the *Pfarrer?*" I asked, aghast.

"Yes, every word of it!" So I told it, word for word, to my religious superior.

The result was "cold war" between the priest and Rudy, with me in the middle of it.

I finally stepped into the battle on my fiancé's side. I went to the bishop for permission to be married. Several influential parents recommended my petition; and the bishop, after we had paid some money and sworn that our children would be reared in the Catholic faith, gave his blessing and the needed signature. Rudy was triumphant; now the priest had to marry us.

Our wedding became a community affair. Pupils and parents showered us with gifts and attention. All my small pupils strewed flowers and lined the isles with lighted candles as we entered the 900-year-old church, filled to the brim with people and flowers, with the smell of incense filling the air. With a face of stone the priest united us. Rudy felt too happy to be mean and was more than willing to bury the battle ax, but the priest was not.

Beginnings?

After an elaborate dinner, my husband and I danced the wedding dance according to an old Bavarian custom, while the other people formed a large circle and watched. When we finished our waltz, the rest of the dancers joined us. Long after we had left the dance floor, we could still hear the music of the brass band and the stomping of many feet, clear into the early morning. Yes, it had been a gala occasion for everybody. Villagers talked about the *Schulfräulein's* wedding for a long time.

We had no honeymoon; Rudy had to return to the university after the weekend, and I continued teaching. He did not like to leave me every Monday morning, because my health began to fail again. I became frightfully thin and pale and began to fear the darkness. The priest had not stopped his antagonism, and life seemed to get more and more difficult. Rudy and I had a hard time adjusting to our new way of life. We both tried hard, but slipped deeper into misunderstandings and estrangement. After our first year of marriage, which was a nightmare, I was convinced I had made a mistake in marrying Rudy. Maybe I had no potential as a good wife; maybe we were just incompatible. I thought I had found a new beginning, but it seemed only the beginning of a bitter end. Rudy and I were ready to give up.

Day of Sunshine

Rudy was desperate. His love for me seemed to deepen in proportion to our insoluble difficulties. If only that priest would stop fighting. I was getting tired of it all.

My classroom was my refuge and haven of peace. My pupils and I understood each other. We loved each other, harmonized with each other. This was all I wanted. The rest of life was agony, friction, pressure.

Rudy had left the house after a rough weekend, as usual, to walk to the railroad station several kilometers from the school. His heart was heavy. He wanted to save our marriage, but it seemed hopeless. We lived in two different worlds and couldn't fit them together. Our ethical principles clashed constantly. His ideas about life and success differed widely from mine.

Until our marriage, Rudy had led an unusual life. After a short time in a prisoner-of-war camp he had established himself on the black market as a cigarette trader. His knowledge of the English language helped. He bought cigarettes for one German mark apiece from the Allied soldiers and sold them to nicotine-hungry German customers for five to seven marks. His business had flourished, and he was known in certain circles as the "cigarette king." At times he had thousands of cigarettes stored in his apartment. Never in his life had Rudy done manual labor; it was beneath him.

I hated this illegal business and insisted that a hard day's honest work never degraded anybody.

On his way to the railroad station Rudy overtook another man. They began to talk, and Rudy generously offered one of his

100

"black" cigarettes. The man, young and seemingly shy, declined politely. Rudy was puzzled. In postwar Germany nobody in his right mind declined a free cigarette. If a person didn't smoke, he still could exchange tobacco for food. Rudy was a chain smoker whose yellow hands trembled from the heavy nicotine intake.

Rudy made an attempt to get the young man to talk. "Did you see the last American movie, which all Munich goes to see?"

"No, I don't go to movies."

"Do you like to dance?" Rudy asked, puzzled.

"No, I don't dance." The other man lapsed into silence.

"Young man, what *do* you like? Maybe your hobby is playing cards at the beer table, or—?"

"No, I don't play cards either, nor do I like beer." He shrugged his shoulders and smiled, obviously a bit amused.

Rudy decided to change the subject. They had passed the home of his old foe, the Catholic priest, and Rudy had to express his resentment toward the *Pfaff* to somebody.

The shy young man, whose name was Sepp, listened patiently. Then he seemed to come alive. Reaching into his coat pocket, he brought forth a small black book, a Bible, and asked, "Did you know, sir, that the doctrines of the Catholic Church are largely based on tradition, not upon the Bible, the only true authority?"

"No, I don't know much about any such thing." Rudy felt uneasy. He did not know which he disliked more, the hated priest or that old Jewish book of fairy tales.

Sepp, who had also bought a ticket back to Munich, was suddenly capable of talking. He introduced himself as a Seventh-day Adventist and began to show Rudy some things about the Bible in relation to the Catholic Church. Rudy became interested, though not in the way Sepp intended. Rudy's quick mind was fast to detect something he had been seeking for a long time. Maybe we could use the Bible as a weapon to fight the Catholic priest, he thought. He began to ask questions. The young man looked pleased at the interest shown and tried to answer; but Rudy's questions demanded deeper answers than Sepp could give. Sepp suggested that Rudy visit the Adventist preacher in the city. He even gave Rudy a letter of introduction, explaining, "I have a heavy tongue like Moses, and I cannot explain things to others as my pastor can."

Rudy was not too enthusiastic about the visit, but his desire for revenge, plus his curiosity, won out. One afternoon when he had no lectures—he was studying law at the university—he set out to find Sepp's preacher. It was not easy. In a poor area of the city, in a basement of a crumbling structure, he found the "office" and the place of worship.

He decided from the beginning not to like it; it smelled and looked too poor for his taste.

The preacher seemed to be pleasant and intelligent. Why would a man like this, and also Sepp, belong to such a ridiculous sect that buried its members alive? No smoke, no drink, no dance, no movies—worshiping in a mousehole under the ground!

The preacher invited Rudy to sit down while he read Sepp's letter. Rudy explained why he had come, making it clear that he had not come to learn about the Adventists. All he wanted were some good smashing arguments to hit the Catholic priest over the head with.

"Mr. Hirschmann," the Adventist minister replied, "I will not be able to help you with your problem. I do not think it would be right for me to give you part of my religion, something very dear and precious to me, something I believe in with all my heart, just to fight a Catholic priest, to get even with somebody. My God, whom I serve, is a God of love!"

Surprised and disappointed, Rudy stood up, shook the preacher's hand, mumbled a thank-you, and managed a polite grin.

"Of course, Mr. Hirschmann," the preacher added as an afterthought, "if you would like to be our guest at our weekly Bible-study class, I could not stop you from making notes which could fit your interest." He handed Rudy a printed invitation which gave the time and place for the different church meetings.

From curiosity and stubbornness, Rudy went. The following

week he sat down in the farthest corner of the room, close to the entrance. The preacher entered, smiled, and greeted everyone individually, then offered a prayer and began to teach.

Rudy was absolutely bored. "*Altweibergeschwätz*, [Old women's tales]!" he fumed. He wondered if he should leave. No, he couldn't be so impolite. After all, he had come of his own free will. Then he heard the preacher mention the Catholic religion. He spoke of the Bible as the Word of God. The man started to read some strange words about a number 666 out of a book called *Revelation*. The speaker brought history into the study, and Rudy began to listen more carefully. History had been his favorite subject since grammar school.

Well, the presentation sounded reasonable, and Rudy had to admit that it made sense. He made careful notes so he would not forget the points needed to embarrass the priest.

Though my husband had no chance to see the priest, he did attend the following Bible study, and the next, and the one after that. He became interested without recognizing it.

"*Schatzi*," he said one day, "those people seem to have something I have never met before. The whole deal leaves me puzzled. How can people be so different? You know, those people have something I want. I mean—not that I want to join that sect—but maybe I can learn enough that it could help me become a better man. After all, dear, I'll do anything to save our marriage, and maybe if we both learn enough about that Christian way of life, we still can make a go of our home!"

I nodded my head in full agreement. "Yes, Rudy, we can at least try it. The things you have heard are not new to me. I was taught that way as a child, only I never mentioned it because I didn't think it would matter to you. But if you want to study more about it, why don't we study together? I have forgotten most of it, but as you tell me certain things, it keeps coming back to my mind. Do you think somebody would be willing to come out and give us studies together?"

To our great surprise the Adventists in Munich agreed to send a minister to our home. But would the minister be willing to come? He had to travel by train, then walk several kilometers through deep snow, stay overnight, and trudge back to the railway station. Who in his right mind would make such efforts just to teach strangers the Bible?

Blessed Brother Schneider! He did it! He came every Friday afternoon, snow, storm, or sunshine, and stepped into the house with the biggest smile I had ever seen. He bore his sixty-five years with dignity and vitality. For months he gave us a Bible study every Friday night, often sitting up with us till late at night. The next morning he had to arise at 4:30 and walk through darkness, ice, and frost to the railroad. Then he traveled into the mountains to serve a small band of believers on Sabbath morning.

Nothing he could have said impressed us as much as this cheerful, unpretending Christian service, which we witnessed with continued astonishment.

I felt sorry for that minister though. Rudy had never showed such an interest before, and I couldn't figure him out. He asked Elder Schneider endless, sometimes even stupid, questions. Rudy had realized, after a short time, that his original plans of accepting Christianity would not work. He knew it would have to be all or nothing. Rudy was not willing to surrender all, so he began to look for traps—traps for the preacher.

In a used bookstore Rudy had found an old Bible. He studied that black Book with a passion, even at the expense of his law studies. But the goal of his searching was not to know God, but to prove that nice man wrong and call the whole deal off.

Elder Schneider! Kind, patient man of God! How I thank you for bearing with us so long! Whenever Rudy asked a question, that old warrior of God stood his ground. With a pleasant smile he replied, "Why don't you open your Bible to—" giving a text and asking one of us to read it aloud. Then we had the answer. I never stopped marveling at the man's knowledge of the Bible. He never used his own arguments or interpretations. The Bible spoke alone, interpreting itself text by text.

Day of Sunshine

During those months our marriage had gone from bad to worse, and so had my health. Rudy battled with himself, with the world, and with God. As Elder Schneider had introduced us week after week to truths that could not be disproved by Rudy's arguments, deep conviction had begun to settle in our hearts.

Winter began to give way to spring, and our faithful teacher walked through slush and ice water in his old, leaky shoes to give us another lesson. I worried that the dear old man would end up with pneumonia for our sake. But he just smiled, dried his shoes and socks at the hearth, and began to teach.

Building upon Christ, the center of all his teaching, he asked us how a child or pupil shows his love toward a parent or teacher.

"Simple," I answered, "by obedience and kindness."

"Right!" answered Pastor Schneider. "God has the same concept. 'If you love Me, keep My commandments.'"

Step by step we were led toward the question of the seventh-day Sabbath. Rudy argued furiously while I listened. I knew who was right. I still had memories of childhood and Sabbath observance, and as the two men talked, the past came back into focus. There was Mother again in sunset worship, and Sabbath School and church services in our humble home. I remembered sitting beside my mother and repeating the Ten Commandments.

"Remember the Sabbath day, to keep it holy—"

Yes, I knew about Sunday too. During my catechism classes with the priest I had asked him about Sunday observance. He had given me precise answers: Yes, the Catholic Church had changed the Sabbath to Sunday at the Council of Laodicea (Canon 29). It had been incorporated into the law of the church in A.D. 451 that Sunday, the festival of resurrection, must be observed in place of the "Judaizing" Sabbath. The priest assured me that this change is proof of the Catholic Church's authority to speak for God on this earth. The priest's reasoning had satisfied me.

Now, as I listened to Elder Schneider while he quoted, as

105

usual, from his beloved Bible, my heart stormed. It was not a question of believing, for I knew he was right. I was willing to believe in God, accept Christ as my Saviour, acknowledge my sins, repent, pray; but to keep the Sabbath was more than all of these other things. It was impractical, actually impossible for me as a teacher. It was ridiculous.

I interrupted, "Brother Schneider, you are right that Saturday is the seventh day, but you know that to keep it is impractical, almost impossible. Take my case, for instance. I teach from Monday morning to Saturday noon. I would lose my job, my apartment, my income, everything, if I didn't teach on Saturday. Rudy would have to stop his studies at the university if my income stops. We would have to begin all over. We would lose all security, and our last few years of work and studies would be wasted. You don't believe *that* would be sensible!"

The minister smiled. It was a warm, understanding smile. "Mrs. Hirschmann, if you believe in God, and believe that the Sabbath is His day, why don't you let God lead, and simply obey?"

"I'll tell you what I will do," I replied. "I will close my school next Saturday and you, sir, *you* take the responsibility!"

That would put him back in his place. I felt good about my quick-witted reply.

"Sister," the preacher said, undisturbed, "I never could take such a responsibility. But" he pointed solemnly toward heaven— "there is Someone up there who will take that responsibility. Go ahead and do it!"

I gulped, ashamed before such a display of sincerity and honest faith. For his sake I had no choice. "OK, I will do it next week, and we shall see what happens!"

Rudy, though yet uncertain of his own convictions, backed me up. The next week I announced with slightly shaking knees that we would have no more school on Saturday.

The pupils looked surprised at first, then became hilariously happy. I dismissed an excited class that day, eager to go home and announce the new "holiday" at the end of every week.

Day of Sunshine

It was different with me. I held my breath and waited for the storm. It had to come, from every side—parents, my supervisor, the *Bürgermeister*, the priest. What would happen? God, are you really there? Will you help?

I couldn't believe it. The storm did not come! The parents were delighted. Farm hands were so short that the children were needed badly at home. A free Saturday meant help, cheap labor to relieve the hardworking adults from many tasks which children can do. The farmers appreciated my decision and let me know about it. The *Bürgermeister* had a fine ear for public opinion and chimed in sweetly with the people. My supervisor chose not to know that he had a school in his district which broke the tradition and rule of the land. My school was, to my knowledge, the only one in all Bavaria that closed its doors on Saturdays.

As the weeks slipped by, free Saturdays became a habit with the community, and people ceased to think much about it. Not so with me. I waited and wondered from week to week, from Sabbath to Sabbath. How long could such a situation exist?

In my heart a little plant had begun to grow. Oh, it was tiny and fragile at first! The plant's name was faith, and God had put it there, through Elder Schneider. From Sabbath to Sabbath that plant grew a little bit more as I learned to wait upon God.

After Elder Schneider had finished his series of studies, he no longer came. Rudy had not made any decisions yet, but he read his Bible regularly, and we often talked and discussed puzzling questions. Our searching and reading had improved our marriage to the extent that we decided to wait awhile with our divorce. We no longer denied that there is a personal God who cares and is able to help. There was that weekly miracle of the closed school door, another thing that reminded us of His interest and care, almost daily.

Something else had happened shortly after we began to keep the Sabbath, before Elder Schneider finished his lessons with us. He had presented the laws of health, and his explanations made sense! If God saw fit in Israel's time to counsel His people against

107

certain articles of diet, these things were not good then and would not be the best for us today. We already understood the harmfulness of alcohol and nicotine, and Rudy had stopped smoking and drinking beer. I didn't care for them anyway. But when it suddenly came to everyday meals and to pork, Rudy's favorite meat, this again came too close for comfort.

Well, we could give it a try! It was Rudy's semester vacation, and he remained at home for two weeks. Since I had to teach in two shifts, I had only forty-five minutes off at lunch, and we ate our meals at the inn across from my school. Food was scarce. Our ration cards never seemed to stretch far enough, but luckily the innkeeper's wife was my friend. She was deeply bothered by our skinniness and tried in a motherly way to fatten both of us up with "extras" on our daily plates. We appreciated our good fortune. After the months of hunger and privation we remembered so vividly, food seemed to be the most important thing in life.

Would God worry about such things? If we tried to stay off unclean food, would He provide our daily bread? Did such rules apply in postwar Germany? We still didn't know God very well; we had only heard about Him from Elder Schneider.

We resolved not to eat unclean food anymore! With that resolution we marched bravely into the inn's small dining room and waved cheerily to our friend the innkeeper's wife. She motioned me to come into the kitchen.

"Luck is with us," she whispered. "My husband found a sow on the black market. He killed it this morning, and we will have additional meat for several weeks. Be careful not to mention it to anyone though."

I managed a half smile and walked in a daze out of the kitchen to sit beside Rudy.

He noticed my stunned expression, and I whispered the big news to him. What should we do? Was *that* God's answer to our decision?

We asked if we could take our plates to our apartment. Our cook loaded the plates generously with pork chops, a small potato, and a spoonful of sauerkraut, and we walked home. We still did not know what to do as we sat at our kitchen table and said the blessing.

Our Russian shepherd puppy, who seemed eternally hungry, sniffed the air. I fed him one piece after another of my food while tears rolled down my face. The pupils were already running above us in the classroom, and I had to go back to my teaching in less than thirty minutes. I was hungry. There was no other food in the house, and we had no time to get any. Besides, our innkeeper kept both our ration cards because we had full provision at his place.

Just then we heard a cackling noise. Months ago one of my pupils had given us two little chickens and some grain to feed them. I kept those chickens in the schoolhouse storage room, hoping to get some eggs someday. Finally we had given up hope and intended soon to fry those skinny hens. Well, for the first time in their young lives I heard them cackle.

Curiously I went out to look. There in the box of straw lay two small eggs, as one hen announced her accomplishment loudly and proudly. Rudy had come out after me, and for a moment we looked into each other's eyes. Each of us knew what the other was thinking. Was this God's answer? Was it a lucky coincidence? Would God really bother to time two eggs for us when we were without food? No minutes left to worry. I ran inside, fixed both eggs, ate happily, and ran up to my classroom.

Those hens laid two eggs every day for several weeks. By that time the sow was used up at the inn, and the menu returned to beef. This brought our home cooking to a happy end. Now we had a song in our hearts, for we knew that the great God of the universe cared for our daily needs.

It took Rudy a while to surrender his heart, but by the time summer had come he was ready.

Shall I ever forget the day? The train had taken us to the city, and we walked to the big public bathhouse beside the river, where the church had rented the pool. Two ministers baptized at the same time. Rudy and I walked together into the water and the ministers baptized us at the same moment. As we came up from the watery grave, we heard the choir sing.

Rudy took my hand and together we walked up the steps, too full of deep emotions to speak. After we had changed into dry clothing, we received the church members' warm welcome.

I looked up into the blue sky and the bright afternoon sunshine. It seemed that I was awakening from a long, oppressive dream. Where had I been until then? There had been so much darkness and fear. Did I have the right to step suddenly into so much light?

Sunbeams sparkled in Rudy's eyes. Squeezing my hand, he said mischievously, "Come on, *Sister* Hirschmann, let's go home!"

Love Unlimited

Baptism was not a wonder cure for all our problems and ills. Clouds still obscured the sun at times. We had been fighting for so long that it had become a habit. Did we stop all at once? Of course not! Sweet old Brother Schneider, so kind and patient, must have foreseen such a thing, for he left us some simple advise: "When you *have* to disagree, remember God's advice for you. 'Let not the sun go down on your wrath.' Do not go to sleep until you forgive each other. Then kneel down and talk to God about it."

We followed his advice, and it saved our marriage. Rudy and I were so different that before we became Christians we had not a chance in the world of getting along with each other. I was a hothead, quick-tempered and volatile, but quickly appeased after the storm.

Rudy was quiet. He chose every word deliberately with time and care. It took him a long time to get upset, and just as long to calm down afterward. Poor husband! I was a nagger by nature and by choice. How often did we have to kneel down those first few months after our spiritual rebirth, pray ourselves together again, and start anew the next morning.

There need be no such thing as incompatibility in a Christian marriage. If any couple was incompatible, we were. We were as different as day and night in every aspect needed for a successful marriage. But we made it by observing that one rule—we prayed together every evening. This sounds too simple, but it worked.

From week to week we learned new things. Sabbath after Sabbath we saw God work, for my school was closed every

111

Saturday for a year and a half. Almost breathlessly we waited from one week to the next for the expected blow. I often wondered why the Lord held the storm down for so long and let us go on waiting and wondering. Years later I understood.

The priest tried everything in his power to get me out of the school and his community. He went to many places, wrote many letters, and preached against us from the pulpit on Sundays. As the months dragged on, I had to watch a heart-tearing thing. The school community split into two camps. One side was the priest's camp, the other that of *Frau Lehrer* (Mrs. Teacher). The controversy raged in homes and at the beer tables of the inn and even entered my classroom, dividing neighbors and friends.

I was sick at heart about it, and my stomach began to act up again. Slowly I lost my new-found smile and peace of mind. After much soul-searching and prayer I decided to turn in my resignation. The reason I gave: poor health.

My supervisor accepted it kindly, and we prepared to leave. Where would we go? Postwar Germany had no housing to offer, no furniture, no freedom to move from one place to the next without permission of the housing commission. Only fools would do what we had done, and we were told so by those who cared enough to advise us, especially by Rudy's parents, who had come to live with Annemarie in the neighboring village. Why throw away a promising job, acceptance in the community, and a nice, warm school apartment, and take to the refugee road again? Rudy's father was especially upset. That crazy new religion! Who would have thought that his only son, the bearer of the proud family name, would do anything so peculiar? No doubt it was his wife who had made him so different. Well, had not the parents known all along?

The storm had begun, and I didn't feel capable of handling it. I was bent over with the pain in my ulcered stomach, undernourished and nervous, depressed and in tears most of the time. Then the doctor told us that our first baby would arrive in due time.

Love Unlimited

In the spring we moved into an attic room of an old farmhouse. A brick chimney that stood in the middle of the room spread heat three times a day, whenever the farmer downstairs made a fire. This was a blessing while the weather was cool, but not when summer came.

Rudy stopped his studies at the university at Munich. Knowing he had to support a wife and soon a baby also, he went out looking for a job. I stayed in our little room, praying and waiting.

What lonely days! It would have been wiser for us to leave the community, but we couldn't because the housing authorities would not transfer us. Besides, in the city with large sections in ruins, it would have taken a lot of money to bribe a landlord to rent us a place to stay.

Every evening Rudy came home weary and discouraged. He could not find a job with so many odds against him. He was a refugee with a Prussian accent, and refugees were not in demand, especially *Saupreussen* (Bavarian slang for Germans from the north). Besides, as a former Nazi officer, the American military government watched him closely. No former Nazi must be allowed to make a comeback in the civil service. Rudy had no references or, for that matter, experience in any trade but fighting. His identification card classified him as a university student, and employers shied away from training students for a trade. Students didn't usually stay long enough to make the training worthwhile, but returned to school as soon as possible.

These odds would have been enough to crush anybody, but on top of it all, Rudy would not work on Saturday. That was it! Rudy could find no job whatever—not even ditchdigging or street sweeping.

After several weeks Rudy began to get desperate. I had tried to keep a smile on my face; but the new life within me was growing, and I anxiously counted the weeks till our baby's birth.

We lived as frugally as possible, but our few marks' savings melted away like snow in the spring sun. One morning we had to sit down and face facts. We counted our money. We had six

113

marks ($1.50) left. Besides our own money, we had some paper notes in an old white envelope. It wasn't much, but it seemed like a large sum because we had almost nothing else. It was our tithe. We had saved it up for many months. We had not turned it in to our church treasury, mainly because we seldom attended church in the city.

That morning I brought the envelope out after we had counted our own last few marks and laid it beside the money box. Somehow, managing to hold my tears back, I said: "Remember what Elder Schneider told us about the tithe? It is God's money, and we must never touch it, not even when in need. He said the truth and we know it. Now, Rudy, the moment our money is gone we shall be tempted to touch what belongs to God, so we must not keep it under our roof any longer. You must take the morning train to the city, find the church treasurer, and give her the money."

Rudy nodded, and his sad eyes revealed what he was thinking. Before he left we knelt together in prayer, and this was the gist of it:

Lord, we have come to the end of our road. We have given up everything we had for our new belief, and it seems that Thou hast forsaken us. If we have done wrong and this is our punishment, please show us why we are punished, because we don't know why! God, maybe we have believed a lie, made up by men. Maybe there is no God and nobody hears us as we pray. But if Thou art, oh, God, reveal Thyself soon, for we cannot go on much longer. Everyone laughs at us already, and our own relatives think we have gone crazy. Oh, Lord, if Thou art, bring help soon and listen to our pleading, for we ask in the name of Thy Son Jesus, in whom we now believe. Amen.

We rose from our knees with heavy hearts, but I smiled and waved to Rudy as he walked away. Then, as soon as he was gone I threw myself on my bed and sobbed. Maybe Rudy's father was right. Maybe it was all my fault. Rudy had accepted our new religion first of all because he loved me and wanted to save our marriage. Sure, he believed in God, but somehow his whole religious experience was tied to his love for me. I felt a great responsibility, since Rudy expected me to lead out in spiritual matters. Alas! Somewhere I had made a mistake, for I had led Rudy and our marriage to a dead-end road, or so it seemed. My heart cried to God, and my tears mingled with my prayers. Doubts and darkness pressed in on me like a fog. Six more weeks before the baby was due, and nothing was ready—nothing was left for us. Oh, God, why?

When Rudy returned, I tried to be brave and calm for his sake, and even managed a smile when he stepped in.

To my amazement, Rudy's face was one big smile. "What happened, dear?" I asked, hardly daring to believe my eyes.

"*Liebling* [darling], I found a job today." Rudy took me in his arms.

Fighting the bothersome tears back, I begged for details.

Rudy said he had battled with temptation and discouragement as he walked the long kilometers to the railroad station and traveled to the city. He had prayed earnestly and had gone straight to the church office to find the lady who managed the church finances. He was afraid to keep our tithe money in his pocket while searching for work again.

The lady, surprised and pleased when Rudy handed her the money, asked the usual questions about our well-being. Rudy told her about our coming baby and his great need for a job.

"Wait a few moments." The kind woman picked up the telephone and made several calls. Then she turned to Rudy. "Brother Hirschmann, I think we have found a job for you. Go to this address right away and ask for Mr. Bauer."

She wrote an address on a piece of paper and handed it to Rudy. He was too surprised to say much, but managed to thank the dear woman warmly before he hurried away.

Mr. Bauer interviewed Rudy briefly and hired him.

"Think of it, dear," Rudy reflected. "For so many weeks I have looked everywhere to find work, but not until we had turned in

115

our tithe was God able to help us. It took only half an hour after I had turned in our tithe to find that job. Now I know God lives and cares!"

We prayed a different prayer that night, a prayer of thanksgiving and praise. Not even the oppressive heat of our attic room bothered us, so happy were we. We sat at the open window and watched the glimmering stars while our hearts conversed with God.

"God," I pleaded humbly, "forgive my doubts; for now I know that Thou art; and not only that, but God, Thou art love."

The stars seemed to smile as they twinkled. They reminded me of the time when Rudy and I had first met, and we had sat on that log to watch our friends, the stars. Then love had begun to bind our hearts together, and now love was again weaving. But this time it was greater love, for God was in it.

Rudy's new job was not very good, but what did it matter? Rudy was willing to do almost anything, and I was willing to pinch the pennies. For the first time in his life the only son of the rich Hirschmann house did manual labor. He had to wrap packages from morning to evening and then deliver the packages to the railway terminal. The factory in which he worked manufactured sport and ski clothing. The company owner had once been a European ski champion, whose name, plus the quality of his merchandise, helped the company grow. The number of packages increased, and Rudy often had to work overtime.

Our baby had arrived too. We named her Christel. The cutest girl who ever arrived on this globe, naturally, she was so tiny that people seemed to see only her long dark hair, big brown eyes, and long, dark eyelashes. We had named her after Rudy's mother, and the grandparents were so delighted about her that they could talk of little else. We soon realized we could not leave the baby in that hot attic room or we might lose her, so when the grandparents offered to take the child and care for her, we accepted, though it was hard to give her up.

116

Rudy's boss had offered us a tiny storage room on the top floor of the factory as sleeping quarters, because the long train trip was difficult when Rudy had to work overtime. We accepted gratefully. Since the baby was in good hands, we could leave our chimney-attic room and the old farmhouse. We carried our few belongings to the city, furnishing our new room with two army cots and some boxes. We felt very fortunate.

After a few weeks of intense search, I found a job in a coat factory and was promoted to office work after a short time. With both of us working, we were soon able to buy ourselves bicycles and also pay the grandparents more for care of the baby. Every weekend we bicycled long miles to see our little daughter for a few short hours. Returning Sunday night, I would lie in bed unable to sleep, my heart aching with longing for my Christel girl. Again prayer helped relieve the loneliness and helped me to learn patience.

Autumn came, with shorter days and longer nights. We had not anticipated problems, but one Friday evening we realized that a new test had arrived. The sun was setting earlier from week to week, and we knew we had to do something about it. Friday night was the busiest for Rudy's work. The company did not work on Saturday, but work was usually not finished on time on Friday, and employees had to stay overtime. Since shipping was the last thing of a long line of tasks, Rudy could never leave until the others had finished.

Friday evening, after sunset, is Sabbath just as much as the next morning, when we have Sabbath School and church. Rudy decided to talk to Mrs. Bauer. She was a member of the *Ostgemeinde* (East Church) to which we belonged, and Rudy had gotten his job through her. Her husband, favorable toward Adventists but not a member of the church, was clerk of the company where Rudy worked. It was Mr. Bauer who made the decisions in matters of employment. We hoped that Mrs. Bauer would talk to her husband first, so he would listen sympathetically when Rudy later approached him.

I Changed Gods

Mrs. Bauer promised to talk with her husband, but after a few days she came back to Rudy, all upset. "Brother Hirschmann," she said urgently, "don't you dare ask my husband for Friday night off. It is impossible to arrange, and if you insist, they will fire you! You will not only lose your job, but your room also, and where would you and your wife go?"

Yes, where would we go? With no living quarters available in the city, we would have to go back where we came from. If we had no place to stay, I would lose my office job also. Could we risk *all* of it just to obey the letter of the law? We prayed about it and young friends in the church prayed also. The more we prayed, the stronger we were convinced that we must stay true to our deep convictions.

One late afternoon Rudy waited until the clerk was all alone and seemingly unhurried. Then, with a soft feeling in his knees, Rudy walked up to the desk and simply asked the boss if he could leave before sunset every Friday night. The clerk looked Rudy up and down in silence. Rudy thought he knew what was coming, and he was prepared for it.

"Yes, Mr. Hirschmann, you may leave by sunset to keep your Sabbath holy!"

Rudy gulped. He was utterly speechless.

Managing a mumbled expression of thanks, Rudy left the office and leaped up the stairs to our room. (I was already back from my work.) He *had* to tell me right away. This was plainly another miracle. Together we knelt and thanked God, not forgetting to ask for a special blessing for his boss and the company. Then Rudy returned to finish his work for the day, whistling and humming happily as he wrapped boxes. People around him looked up. "What happened to you today, Rudy? Did you win a lottery prize or inherit a fortune?"

"No! Something much better," answered my usually reserved husband, beaming, "I have seen God work a miracle!"

Rudy left on Friday before sunset. When he came down the following Monday morning, the owner of the company waited for him. The clerk had given permission to Rudy, but had wisely not informed the owner of that new arrangement. But the owner had found out, and was fuming so that not even the Bavarian language gave him adequate means of expression. He called Rudy a loafer, a hypocrite, and a sucker, and climaxed the tirade by threatening to fire him if he left work the next Friday or any other Friday.

Rudy felt his knuckles tightening. Never before in his life had anybody talked like that to him. Rudy had given orders for many years; to be treated like a servant was a new experience, a hard one. But Rudy managed to keep his mouth tightly shut. After the boss had stomped off, he went quietly to his place of work. He called me during lunch hour, promising to leave the following Friday before sunset regardless of the consequences. I assured him I was in full agreement.

As the week wore on we prayed; and other church members joined in.

Before sunset Rudy left inconspicuously. He knew word had spread among the other employees, and everybody was watching the developing battle between employee and employer.

The following Monday the boss was waiting again. He had somehow found some stronger language yet, and his voice had become louder too. The employees listened while the lion roared. The same threat topped the lecture, while Rudy stood in silence and listened.

Rudy left every Friday before sunset. Every Monday morning before he went downstairs for work he would say, "*Schatzi*, have things ready. I might really be fired today."

The boss threatened, yelled, scolded through the entire winter. Sometimes it seemed more than Rudy was able to bear from week to week. Again, prayer saw us through those months.

During those months we saw Mr. Bauer come to our church with his wife more regularly. One day she said quietly, "Since we are watching the happenings around you two young, newly baptized kids, my husband is much more interested in our religion.

119

The Lord is truly with you and is making the heart of the boss like a river of water. Remain faithful; God is using you for witnesses!"

Spring came, and the days lengthened again. Rudy was able to work Fridays until closing time, and the boss had found his composure again. Some church members felt that we had gone too far, for the boss announced to anyone who wanted to know that he would *never* employ another Seventh-day Adventist. Had we spoiled other Adventists' chances for employment because we tried too eagerly to fulfill the letter of the law? Were we like the Pharisees of Jesus' time?

We had only the Bible and our conscience to go by. The Bible seemed like a huge map, and the main road to heaven was marked clearly. But we sometimes longed for the small landmarks and detailed instructions fitted for our modern times, because so many church people had different ideas and opinions. Some people prayed for us and encouraged us, while others criticized. We were often confused and bewildered. We had been told that God had left very specific and detailed instructions for all of us in the spirit of prophecy writings, but we could not get any of those books then. We had to go by hearsay as the older church members told us what the books said.

One day in late spring Rudy was called into the office.

"What did I do now?" he asked.

The owner and the clerk offered him a chair. "Our company is planning to export ski clothing to America and other countries," the owner began, "and Mr. Bauer has recommended you as manager of the new export department. Would you be interested?"

Rudy was not sure if he had heard right. "Did you say *I* have been considered for export management?"

"What else? Do you think you can do it?"

Rudy thought fast. "Yes, I think I could, only I will not work on my Sabbath, including Friday nights during winter."

"We know that already." The boss sounded irritated. "But we shall give it a try and see if it works out."

They discussed new wages and other details, and an overjoyed husband arrived home that night.

The pay was two and a half times what he had earned as a packer—and a church member had just offered us a basement apartment in his house.

While Rudy began to build up his new export department from nothing, I began to set up our first real household the same way. Then came the happy day when we could bring our child home. She was two years old, and had never seen the city. After a few weeks of readjustment she was happy again and filled our lives with a new joy and happiness. She liked Sabbath School and impressed the old sisters of the church with her model behavior. Christel was like her daddy—quiet, reserved, and gentle—and she became a favorite child to many. How proud we were to show her off!

Yes, things were brightening up for us, and besides, Rudy found a little house for rent on the outskirts, close to the new plant the company was building.

Christel's little brother had just arrived. With prayers of thankfulness we moved out of the city into that cute little house with its garden and big evergreen tree. The new baby had fresh air and sunshine, and Christel played for many hours beside his basket.

Rudy's department had grown to such an extent that in the busy season he had eight people working under him. He and Mr. Bauer had become very good friends, and in free moments they often discussed the Bible and its doctrines. Mr. Bauer had started to come regularly to church. He attended my Sabbath School class. Rudy and I had grown active in the church, and we carried several church offices.

Just as everything was going so well, another "bomb" exploded. The company owner received a letter from his largest export customer in the United States, announcing his arrival the following Saturday.

"I expect you to be here and serve that man," growled the

owner. "You speak English; it is your responsibility, and it's only once. Tell your preacher to excuse you from church service for that day!"

Rudy shook his head. "I am sorry, sir. I will not be able to be here next Saturday, even if my minister approved it. You see, I obey God, not man!"

"And what do you suggest?" sputtered Rudy's boss. "Am I supposed to cancel my skiing appointment with my friends because of *your* religion? Or do we tell that American visitor we cannot receive him because my company was foolish enough to employ a Seventh-day Adventist in the export department?"

"Sir," said Rudy in his quiet way, "at present I have no solution to the problem. But we can pray to God about it!"

The boss looked ready to throw Rudy out. "You and your silly old-woman prayers!" He handed Rudy the letter. "Here! Take care of it, and we shall see what your God can do!"

We prayed as never before, as we wanted to be sure we were using faith, not presumption. Would God honor Rudy's faith before his boss, or was Rudy boasting and needlessly putting God "on the spot"? As usual we asked our friends to join us in our petitions to God.

Friday came, and we had not solved the problem. Rudy left solemnly after morning prayer, knowing he was again close to being fired. I kept on praying as I prepared for the Sabbath and tried hard not to worry.

One hour before sunset, as Rudy was finishing things up so he could leave, the telephone rang and Rudy answered it. It was an American calling from Hamburg: "Mr. Hirschmann, I have an appointment with you tomorrow morning to see your merchandise. I am very sorry, but I can't make it tomorrow. Would you be nice enough to see me Sunday morning instead?"

Would he! Rudy would be *delighted* to meet him on Sunday. After the gentleman had hung up, Rudy hurried to the office of his boss and told him the news, adding, "Sir, can you see *how* God is able to answer prayer?"

The owner smiled. "Well, yes, it was a lucky accident. But who will be here on Sunday?"

"Sir," Rudy offered, "I will be delighted to be here and serve that man. Sunday is my first workday of the week!"

Things happened that way several times after that, so the owner could see that the incidents were not merely lucky accidents. The Lord never let Rudy down, but blessed and guided marvelously. Rudy was well on his way to success—financial security, a car, and a lifetime job. The boss couldn't help agreeing when Mr. Bauer pointed out that God was blessing the export department. This was plainly visible.

Could we ask for any more than we had? Had not God led all the way? Were not His hands pointing toward faithful service in Rudy's new profession as a respectable business manager?

Since 1945 I had cherished a dream, and later Rudy dreamed it with me. We wanted to go to America! Alas! It would have to remain a dream; we had no chance to go.

Shortly after we became Seventh-day Adventists we applied through the Church World Service for a sponsor and a loan to go to the land of our dreams. The sponsor had been found and the loan approved. Our hopes had risen especially during that dreadful winter when Rudy almost lost his job from one Monday to the next. But the visa for our immigration did not come through. Some of our best refugee friends had already left for the United States and had written glowing letters about the abundant food and housing there. Several of our requests to the American consulate went unanswered, and we slowly gave up hope. Then one day in 1951 we received a letter announcing that a CIC officer would visit us. We were puzzled. I tried to shine up our humble home to be presentable for such a guest.

The uniformed man came. After a short interview we learned that they knew all about our military training. He said he was sorry to inform us that we had little chance to enter America. Rudy had been engaged in active warfare against the United

States, and the law forbade entrance to former officers like Rudy. Rudy nodded. Yes, he had fought against the United States. Twice he had surfaced near Florida, once close enough to see the lights of Miami. It had been his business to sink ships, and he had done a good job of it. Now he had to pay the price for it. All right, so we could not go to the United States.

I couldn't understand a word of the English spoken, so Rudy translated for me.

"Rudy," I said softly in German, "why did the man come, if we cannot go to America? Did he come only to announce *that* to us?"

The American understood what I had asked Rudy, and explained: Since Rudy had served on one of the German *snorkel* boats the United States Government might waive its objections. It was looking for men with Rudy's kind of experience for research in the defense machinery of the United States. It was understood that Rudy would receive a good salary and enjoy a high standard of living.

Rudy looked at me. He knew how much I wanted to go to the States. This was the opportunity of our life.

"Sir," Rudy replied, "I wish to thank you for your offer. I feel honored and would be pleased to give the United States my service. But after the war my wife and I became Seventh-day Adventists. My religion teaches me not to kill. I do not wish to work in connection with war, killing, and shooting."

"But, Mr. Hirschmann, you don't have to fight or kill. You will be actually helping to preserve peace. You know how it is with Uncle Joe [Stalin]; the free world has to be on guard!" The man smiled encouragingly.

Rudy shook his head. "I am sorry, sir, but my conscience cannot accept your offer. I have seen too much of death and sorrow. I do not feel that I should ever have anything to do with war again."

The officer stood up, obviously puzzled, even angry. He gave our dilapidated surroundings one more supercilious look. "You will *never* see the United States of America," he said and left.

I could not help crying after Rudy told me what was said. Dreams are like rainbows—they brighten dark clouds and build bridges into the sky. When dreams die, the earth looks sad.

After I had cried awhile, I wiped my tears and smiled at Rudy. Why worry? Was not God leading our lives? That night I knelt by my bed and prayed and then climbed into my bed. "Rudy," I said, "deep inside I have a feeling that we shall go to America someday, whenever it is time for us, and we shall serve God in America. Let's wait and see!"

Rudy reached over and squeezed my arm. "Little Hansi, your optimism is something wonderful! Keep hoping and praying."

Years passed, and our dreams of America grew dim. Maybe it had been wishful thinking and not God's assurance. Maybe our place was in Germany. People advised us against trying to go to the strange New World. Rudy's parents were horrified. Give up a promising job and cross the ocean into the unknown? Stupid! My foster mother, whom I had found one year after the war ended, and who had been so happy about our baptism, wrote me loving letters with many words of caution. Finally I gave my dream up and settled down for good.

Then the Lord began to open the door. Laws had been changed in the United States. Friends found a sponsor, and the Church World Service offered us a loan. Before we knew it, we had our home disposed of and two suitcases packed. One suitcase held the most necessary clothing for our two children and ourselves; the second was filled with books, new and used, which had become too precious to part with.

The last Sabbath before the flight I went to see my mother. She lived with one of her daughters who had found a new home in southern Bavaria. It happened that they celebrated the Lord's Supper in her church that day. We had never broken bread together as sisters in Christ, and my heart was full with deep gratitude to God for that privilege. We washed each other's feet, shared the bread and cup, and sat silently together as I held her wrinkled, wilted hand in mine.

I Changed Gods

"Marichen," she whispered softly, "do you have to leave me again?"

"Mother," I replied, "I know it is God's calling for us!"

"If it is God's calling, you must not stay." She wiped her eyes.

I looked into her face. Her eyes were filled with peace and love. When I kissed her for the last time, I knew that this time mother was not worried. There was no anguish, no foreboding of great danger. My mother's God had become my God again, and she sent me away with her blessings.

The many farewells were hard. Love seemed to surround us on every side. Rudy's company gave us a big farewell party. The job left vacant by Rudy had been given to another Seventh-day Adventist. There were nine Adventists employed by the time we left, some of them in key positions. Mr. Bauer, who was taking baptismal classes at the time of our leaving, had tears in his eyes. The owner of the company handed Rudy a check worth $100. Who would have dared to dream of such an ending? Only God could bring so many wonderful things about.

The airplane trip was a new experience for all of us. We climbed higher and higher into clouds and sky. We watched our homeland vanish and saw the vast ocean stretching far below.

Through the long night hours of the flight I wondered, had we done the right thing? Was it really God's calling for us?

Again we had left everything behind us to follow a conviction. We did not know what the future would bring. We did not know our new homeland. We called nothing our own but our two children, two suitcases, and a hundred-dollar check.

Again we had become wanderers between two worlds. Again we had many plans and resolutions for a new beginning. Rudy would go to a Christian college; maybe I would too. We would enter the Lord's work and win many souls. I dreamed and mused as I watched the stars grow dim.

Hope and doubts, trust and fear battled within me. I prayed and struggled, but I did not seem to break through to my God. I looked out and up into the morning sky.

126

My little boy awoke and asked,
"Mommy, is God living up there?"